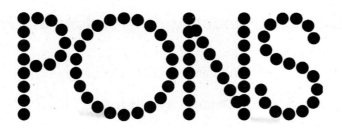

Englische
Handelskorrespondenz
im Griff

von
Rachel Armitage-Amato
Neubearbeitung von
Catherine E. Baker

D1619242

Ernst Klett Verlag
Stuttgart·Düsseldorf·Leipzig

Englische Handelskorrespondenz im Griff

von Rachel Armitage-Amato

Deutsche Bearbeitung
Sigrid Leonard
Neubearbeitung
Catherine E. Baker

Gedruckt auf Papier, das aus chlorfrei gebleichtem
Zellstoff hergestellt wurde.

3. überarbeitete Auflage A3 ³ ² ¹ | 2001 2000 99

Internetadresse: http://www.pons.de

Redaktion: Annie Faugére, Caroline Haydon, Bernard Wall
Einbandgestaltung: Erwin Poell, Heidelberg; Ilona Arfaoui, Stuttgart
Bildquelle Umschlag: Thomas Weccard, Ludwigsburg
Satz: Satz & mehr, Besigheim
Druck: Druckerei zu Altenburg, Altenburg
Printed in Germany
ISBN 3-12-560986-0

INHALTSVERZEICHNIS

THEMEN – *TOPICS*

ANHANG – *REFERENCE SECTION*

SO BENUTZEN SIE DIESES BUCH

Wenn Sie lernen möchten, sämtliche Formen des Schriftverkehrs im Englischen zu beherrschen, so beachten Sie bitte folgende Hinweise:

- Lesen Sie zuerst das Einführungskapitel **allgemeine Regeln**.

In den nachfolgenden Kapiteln lernen Sie dann, wie im Englischen Briefe formuliert werden. Dabei werden Sie häufig der Unterteilung in die beiden Kategorien „formell" und „informell" begegnen, die sich häufig aber nicht immer mit den Kategorien des „Geschäftsbriefes" und des „privaten Briefes" decken. Prinzipiell ist jedes Kapitel folgendermaßen unterteilt:

- Zunächst vervollständigen Sie einen **Lückenbrief**. Hierfür wählen Sie aus einer Liste mit mehreren Angaben den jeweils passendsten Ausdruck und setzen ihn in die entsprechende Lücke ein. Im Anhang des Buches finden Sie den dazugehörigen **Lösungsbrief**, der Ihnen auch als Musterbrief dienen kann.

- Im Abschnitt **Redewendungen** lernen Sie, welche Ausdrücke in bestimmten Situationen gängig sind.

- In den **Anmerkungen** werden Sie auf besondere sprachliche Formen und zu beachtende Schwierigkeiten bei der Übersetzung hingewiesen.

- Schließlich heißt es: „**SIE SIND DRAN !**". In diesem Teil sollen Sie selber mit Hilfe von Lückensätzen, die Sie vervollständigen müssen, eigenständig Briefe aufsetzen. Auf diese Weise merken Sie sich die wichtigsten Begriffe und Wendungen und prägen sich die verschiedenen Formulierungsmöglichkeiten ein. Auch für diese Briefe finden Sie im Anhang Lösungsvorschläge.

Wenn Sie punktuelle Hilfestellung brauchen, können Sie das vorliegende Buch auch als Nachschlagewerk verwenden:

- Im Einführungskapitel **allgemeine Regeln** werden Ihnen die in der englischen Korrespondenz üblichen Formregeln vermittelt.

- Die **Musterbriefe** können als Vorlage dienen, wenn Sie zu einem bestimmten Themenbereich einen Brief schreiben müssen.

- Die **nützlichen Redewendungen** bieten Ihnen einen Abriss der geläufigsten Wendungen der englischen Geschäftskorrespondenz.

- In den **Glossaren** schließlich finden Sie die geläufigsten Begriffe aus dem Bereich der Korrespondenz in deutscher und englischer Sprache.

Und nun: viel Erfolg beim Schreiben …!

ALLGEMEINE REGELN

Im folgenden Musterbrief sehen Sie, wie ein moderner englischer Geschäftsbrief aufgesetzt wird:

LUXI PHON
Magdeburger Straße 250 · 10785 Berlin

Mr J. P. Queensway
Branch Manager
Financial Bank PLC
45 Highway Avenue
Banbury
Kent AP7 5RT   8th January 19...

Our ref: RM / AF 2411
Your ref: JQ / 108

Dear Mr Queensway

Delivery charges

Thank you for your inquiry of 1st January. We hope you will find the enclosed information useful. Thank you once again for the interest shown in our products.

Yours sincerely

R. Maskin

R Maskin (Mrs)

p.p. Mr J Müller
Export Manager

Enc

Unser Musterbrief auf der linken Seite zeigt Ihnen die wohl geläufigste Form der Gestaltung. Da die Regeln im Englischen aber weniger streng sind als im Deutschen, werden Sie auch andere Varianten antreffen.

ADRESSE UND ANSCHRIFT

Bei Firmenpapier mit Briefkopf erscheint die Empfängeradresse auf der linken Seite. Das Datum steht rechts auf gleicher Höhe mit der ersten oder letzten Zeile der Empfängeradresse.

→ Beachten Sie: Wenn das Schreiben keinen Briefkopf hat, erscheint die Empfängeradresse ebenfalls links, aber die des Absenders rechts (s. u.). Das Datum steht dann direkt unter der Absenderadresse und zwar auf gleicher Höhe mit der ersten Zeile der Empfängeradresse:

                                        Luxiphon
                                          Magdeburger Str. 250
                                          10785 Berlin

Hi-Tech Productions Ltd   7th March 19…
Brooks House
56 George Street
Oxford OX1 6PQ

ANREDE IN DER ANSCHRIFT

- **Ms**: für eine Frau, von der nicht bekannt ist, ob sie ledig oder verheiratet ist (Ursprünglich amerikanisches Englisch, diese Anrede setzt sich nun auch im britischen Englisch durch.)
- **Mrs**: für eine verheiratete Frau
- **Miss**: für eine ledige Frau, gilt jedoch zunehmend als veraltet
- **Mr**: für einen Mann
- **Messrs**: für zwei und mehrere Herren

Wenn Sie den Namen des Adressaten nicht kennen, können Sie seine Funktion in der Firma angeben oder die Abteilung (z. B. „Sales Department").

ANREDE AM BRIEFANFANG

Formelle Beziehungen:

Sie schreiben:	Die Anrede lautet:
einer Firma, oder einer Person, von der Sie weder Namen noch Geschlecht kennen.	*Britisches Englisch:* Dear Sir / Madam Dear Sir or Madam *Amerikanisches Englisch:* Dear Sir / Madam Dear Sir or Madam To whom it may concern
einer Frau (verheiratet oder ledig), deren Namen Sie nicht kennen.	Dear Madam
einem Mann, dessen Namen Sie nicht kennen.	Dear Sir
einer Person, deren Namen Sie kennen.	Dear Mr (*bzw.* Mrs / Ms / Miss) Brown

➔ Wundern Sie sich nicht, wenn Ihr englischer Geschäftspartner Sie schon bald im Brief mit Ihrem Vornamen anredet. Dies bedeutet nicht, dass er Sie damit in seinen engsten Freundeskreis aufgenommen hat! Im Englischen geht man einfach nach kürzerer Zeit als im Deutschen zu einem weniger formellen Umgangston über.

Informelle oder persönliche Beziehungen:

Sie schreiben:	Die Anrede lautet:
einer Person, deren Namen Sie kennen.	Dear Mr (*bzw.* Mrs / Ms / Miss) Brown
einer Person, die Sie bereits mit Vornamen anschreibt bzw. anspricht.	Dear Susan / Dear David
einer Freundin / einem Freund.	Dear Carol / Dear John

➔ Diese Anreden wären für eine E-Mail passend.

ABSCHLIESSENDE GRUSSFORMEL

Formelle Beziehungen:

Sie schreiben:

einer Firma (Dear Sir or Madam /
To whom it may concern),
oder
einer Person, von der Sie weder
Namen noch Geschlecht kennen
(Dear Sir / Madam),
oder
einer Person, deren Namen Sie
nicht kennen (Dear Sir /
Dear Madam).

einer Person, deren Namen Sie
kennen (Dear Mr Brown).

Die Grußformel lautet:

Britisches Englisch:
Yours faithfully
Amerikanisches Englisch:
Yours truly
Truly yours

Britisches Englisch:
Yours sincerely
Amerikanisches Englisch:
Yours truly
Very truly yours
Sincerely (yours)

Informelle oder persönliche Beziehungen:

Sie schreiben:

einer Person, deren Namen Sie
kennen (Dear Mr Brown),
oder
einer Person, die Sie bereits mit
Vornamen anschreibt bzw. an-
spricht (Dear Susan).

einer Freundin / einem Freund.

Die Grußformel lautet:

Britisches Englisch:
(With) Best wishes
Regards
Amerikanisches Englisch:
Sincerely (yours)

Britisches Englisch:
(With) Best wishes
Yours
Love
Amerikanisches Englisch:
All the best
Kindest / Best regards
Regards
(With) Best wishes

→ Beachten Sie: Nur das erste Wort in der Grußformel wird groß geschrieben.

→ **Regards** wird häufig als Grußformel in einem Telefax-Schreiben oder in einer E-Mail benutzt.

UNTERSCHRIFT

Die Unterschrift steht immer zwischen der abschließenden Grußformel und dem maschinengeschriebenen Namen des Absenders, dem auch Titel sowie Funktion innerhalb der Firma hinzugefügt werden können:

Yours faithfully

R Maskin (Mrs)
Sales Representative

→ Beachten Sie: Sollte aus dem maschinengeschriebenen Namen nicht eindeutig hervorgehen, ob der Absender männlich oder weiblich ist, so handelt es sich im Allgemeinen um einen Mann.

KURZZEICHEN UND VERMERKE

Sie sind an verschiedenen Stellen im Brief möglich, wie z. B.:

• Oben links, unter dem Briefkopf / Über oder unter der Anschrift:

Ref: – Aktenzeichen des Absenders, das normalerweise aus den Initialen des Verfassers und seiner Sekretärin besteht, sowie einer Aktenziffer, einer Kontonummer oder einer Kundennummer z. B.: SJG / AD 567
Our ref: – Aktenzeichen des Absenders (siehe oben)
Your ref: – Aktenzeichen des Empfängers, das der Absender in seiner Antwort übernimmt

• Nach der Empfängeranschrift:

For the attention of Mr Shaw oder **Attention: Mr Shaw** – um den Namen des tatsächlichen Empfängers hervorzuheben
To whom it may concern (≈ an alle, die es betrifft) – an einen unbekannten Empfänger

• Nach der Anrede:

Water supplies in India – Betreff des Briefes
ACCOUNT No. 556378 – der Brief bezieht sich auf das angegebene Konto
Grant's & Co Ltd – der Brief betrifft die hier zitierte Firma

- Zwischen abschließender Grußformel und Unterschrift / Zwischen Unterschrift und maschinengeschriebenem Namen:

p.p. – in Vertretung; der Unterzeichnende ist rechtlich dazu autorisiert, im Namen der Firma oder für jeden anderen stellvertretend zu unterschreiben

- Unten links, unterhalb der Unterschrift:

PS: – wird in informellen Briefen benutzt um etwas hinzuzufügen, was im Hauptteil des Briefes vergessen wurde
Enc(s) oder **Encl(s)** – weist darauf hin, dass dem Brief Dokumente (Schecks, Kataloge, Kostenvoranschläge etc.) beigefügt sind
cc: oder **copy to:** – bezeichnet die Namen derer, die eine Kopie des Briefes erhalten haben

STIL UND GESTALTUNG

- Bei der Anrede und der Grußformel wird immer häufiger auf Interpunktion verzichtet. Wichtig ist es, konsequent zu sein: also entweder beides mit Kommas am Ende, oder beides ohne Kommas.

Dear Mr Simpson,   Dear Mr Simpson
Yours sincerely,   Yours sincerely

- Der Hauptteil des Briefes beginnt mit der ersten Zeile nach der Anrede und wird heutzutage immer folgendermaßen gestaltet:
  - Alle Zeilen beginnen am linken äußeren Rand, Absätze werden durch Leerzeilen markiert.
  - Das erste Wort im Hauptteil des Briefes, also nach der Anrede, wird in der englischen Korrespondenz immer groß geschrieben.

- Ein Geschäftsbrief muss vor allem einfach sein. Ziehen Sie deshalb kurze Sätze vor.

- Heute darf man die Sätze durchaus mit **I** oder **we** beginnen, vorausgesetzt, man übertreibt es nicht. Komplizierte Strukturen lassen sich dadurch oft vermeiden.

- Vermeiden Sie im Brief Kurzformen wie: „I'd, I'll, won't, don't, can't, haven't" etc. Diese sind normalerweise der gesprochenen Sprache vorbehalten.

- Benutzen Sie, wenn möglich, die 3. Person und das Passiv, z. B. **Your order is being processed** (Ihre Bestellung wird bearbeitet), anstelle von „Someone is processing your order" (jemand bearbeitet Ihren Auftrag).
  Diese Technik bietet die Möglichkeit, in angemessenem Stil im Namen der Firma zu sprechen. Der indirekte Stil lässt sich auch besonders diplomatisch bei Reklamationen oder Absagen verwenden:

A mistake has been made in our order (In unserer Bestellung wurde ein Fehler festgestellt) ist viel höflicher als „You have made a mistake in our order".

- Denken Sie daran, dass E-Mails üblicherweise echt locker formuliert werden. Die Adresse des Absenders im Sinne von einem in Briefen üblichen Briefkopf wird gelegentlich am Ende des Mails angegeben. (Signatur)

UMSCHLAG

- Auf dem Umschlag erscheinen Name und Adresse genau wie in der Anschrift, nur dass Abkürzungen für **Road (Rd)**, **Avenue (Av)** und **Street (St)** benutzt werden können.

- Der Name des Landes wird durchgängig groß geschrieben, die Postleitzahl bzw. der Postcode bekommt eine eigene Zeile:

Mr T Simons
Morvan Manufacturing
Bromsgrove Rd
Sheffield Yorkshire
SF2 5ST
UNITED KINGDOM

Folgende besondere Hinweise können auf dem Umschlag stehen:

Air mail	*Luftpost*
Express	*Eilbrief*
Urgent	*Eilig*
Registered	*Einschreiben*
Private	*Persönlich*
Personal	*Persönlich*
Printed matter	*Drucksache*
Confidential	*Vertraulich*
To be called for	*Postlagernd*
Poste restante	*Postlagernd*
Please forward	*Bitte nachsenden*
Sample	*Muster*
Fragile	*Zerbrechlich*
Postage paid	*Gebührenfrei*

Diese Hinweise stehen in der oberen linken Ecke des Umschlags.

 **SIE SIND DRAN!**

Verbinden Sie jede Anrede mit einer passenden Grußformel.
Achtung: es gibt manchmal mehrere Möglichkeiten! Die Lösungen finden Sie auf
Seite 131. Schlagen Sie aber nicht sofort nach!

Britisches Englisch
Anrede: **Grußformel:**

Dear Sir / Madam   Best wishes

Dear Mr Shaw   Yours faithfully
(Geschäftspartner – formell)

Dear Sarah *(eine Freundin)*   Regards

Dear David   Yours sincerely
(Geschäftspartner – informell)

Dear Mrs Wilks   Yours
(Geschäftspartnerin – informell)

Amerikanisches Englisch
Anrede: **Grußformel:**

Dear Sir / Madam   Yours truly

Dear Mr Shaw   All the best
(Geschäftspartner – formell)

Dear Sarah *(eine Freundin)*   Best wishes

Dear David   Regards
(Geschäftspartner – informell)

Dear Mrs Wilks   Sincerely
(Geschäftspartnerin – informell)

To whom it may concern

1 RESERVIERUNGEN VORNEHMEN

Die Firma Luxiphon stellt Luxustelefone her. Herr Müller wird sie auf der Internationalen Telekommunikationsmesse in Birmingham vertreten. Er bereitet seine Reise vor.

Jens Müller
Magdeburger Str. 250
10785 Berlin

Paradise Hotel   4th February 19...
155 Bourneville Rd
Birmingham B25 S10

(1) _____

(2) _____ (3) _____ a single room at
your hotel (4) _____ of 19th-26th February. (5)
_____ a room with a view of the gardens, a telephone,
and a private bathroom with shower.

(6) _____ my booking (7) _____ , and if you
could (8) _____ your rates per night including breakfast.

(9) _____ , please could you give me the address of a
suitable hotel in the Birmingham area?

(10) _____

J. Müller

J Müller

Brief 1: Lösung auf Seite 131

Helfen Sie ihm eine Hotelreservierung vorzunehmen. (Von den drei vorgegebenen Formulierungen passt jeweils nur eine in den nebenstehenden Lückenbrief.)

(1) *Die Anrede:*
Dear Sir
To Paradise Hotel
Dear Sir / Madam

(2) *Einen Wunsch äußern:*
I require
I would like
I want

(3) *Ein Zimmer „reservieren" heißt:*
to book
to rent
to hire

(4) *Welche ist die passende Präposition?*
in the week
during the week
for the week

(5) *„Ich benötige":*
I require
I would be interested in
It would be nice to have

(6) *Um eine Bestätigung bitten:*
I should be grateful if you
   would confirm
Thank you for confirming
Please register

(7) *Um eine rasche Antwort bitten:*
as soon as possible
very quickly
at your convenience

(8) *Informationen erbitten:*
show me
give me an indication of
give me information on

(9) *„Falls kein Zimmer frei ist":*
Should you have no vacancies
If you haven't got any rooms
If there is no space left

(10) *Die Grußformel:*
Yours faithfully
Best wishes
Yours sincerely

REDEWENDUNGEN

Ein Zimmer suchen

I would like to book... .
I would be interested in booking ... .

Ich möchte ... reservieren.
Ich wäre daran interessiert(,)... zu buchen / reservieren.

I am writing to you (in order) to ... .
I am looking for a suitable hotel near the airport.

Ich schreibe Ihnen(,) um ... zu ... .
Ich suche ein gutes / geeignetes Hotel in Flughafennähe.

Reservieren, buchen, mieten

to book / reserve a single / double room

ein Einzel- / Doppelzimmer reservieren / buchen

I would like to reserve the presidential suite.	Ich möchte die Luxussuite reservieren.
We have booked a table for three.	Wir haben einen Tisch für drei Personen reservieren lassen.
Have you reserved seats for the theatre?	Haben Sie Plätze für das Theater reserviert?
I would like to reserve two seats on the next flight to New York.	Ich möchte zwei Plätze für den nächsten Flug nach New York buchen.
to rent a flat / a room / a car	eine Wohnung / ein Zimmer / ein Auto mieten
to hire a car / a boat / a bicycle	ein Auto / ein Boot / ein Fahrrad mieten

Ein Bedürfnis oder einen Wunsch äußern

I require… .	Ich benötige … .
I will / would require… .	Ich werde / würde … benötigen.
I would be interested in… .	Ich wäre an … interessiert.
I would be grateful for… .	Ich wäre (Ihnen) für … dankbar.
I would be grateful if you would… .	Ich wäre (Ihnen) dankbar, wenn Sie … könnten.
Could you supply me with…?	Könnten Sie mir … besorgen?

Eine Dauer, einen Zeitraum angeben

for the week of 19th-26th February	für die Woche vom 19. bis 26. Februar
for the month of May	für (den gesamten) Mai
for five weeks as from 20th July	für fünf Wochen, ab dem 20. Juli
for this / next / the coming weekend	für dieses / das nächste / das kommende Wochenende
for the Easter / summer holidays	für die Oster- / Sommerferien
from 19th to 26th February	vom 19. bis 26. Februar
from 2nd May onwards	ab dem 2. Mai / beginnend am 2. Mai

Ein Zimmer beschreiben

a room with a view	ein Zimmer mit Ausblick
a room which looks out onto the courtyard / garden	ein Zimmer zum Hof / Garten hinaus
a room which faces the sea	ein Zimmer mit Meeresblick
a south-facing room	ein Zimmer nach Süden
an air-conditioned room	ein klimatisiertes Zimmer
a room…	ein Zimmer …
with bath and shower	mit Bad und Dusche
with air conditioning	mit Klimaanlage
with a child's bed	mit Kinderbett
with plenty of light	das möglichst hell ist

Um eine Bestätigung bitten

I should be grateful if you would confirm… .	*Ich wäre Ihnen dankbar, wenn Sie (mir) … bestätigen könnten.*
Please confirm… .	*Mit der Bitte um Bestätigung … .*
I should be obliged if you would confirm this reservation.	*Ich wäre Ihnen dankbar, wenn Sie diese Reservierung bestätigen könnten.*

Um eine rasche Antwort bitten

as soon as possible	*so bald wie möglich*
by return of post	*postwendend*
at your earliest convenience (gilt als ein wenig veraltet)	*sobald es Ihnen möglich ist*

Nach dem Preis fragen

I would be grateful for an indication of your rates.	*Ich wäre Ihnen dankbar, wenn Sie mir Ihre Preise mitteilen könnten.*
I would like to know your daily / weekly / monthly rates.	*Bitte teilen Sie mir Ihre Tarife pro Tag / Woche / Monat mit.*
Please send us your price list.	*Bitte senden Sie uns Ihre Preisliste.*
I would like to know what you charge for… .	*Was / Wieviel berechnen Sie für …?*

Welche Mahlzeiten sind inbegriffen?

including breakfast	*Frühstück inbegriffen*
evening meal included	*Abendessen inbegriffen*
full board / half board	*Vollpension / Halbpension*
Bed and Breakfast	*Zimmer mit Frühstück*
B & B and evening meal	*Zimmer mit Frühstück und Abendessen*

Falls kein Zimmer frei ist

Should you have no vacancies… .	*Sollten Sie keine Zimmer (mehr) frei haben, … .*
If you have no vacancies… .	*Wenn Sie keine Zimmer (mehr) frei haben … .*
no vacancies	*belegt / ausgebucht*
Should you have no accommodation available… .	*Sollten Sie keine Unterbringungs-möglichkeiten (mehr) haben, :… .*

ANMERKUNGEN

➔ Im Englischen kann man „reservieren" sowohl mit **to reserve** als auch mit **to book** ausdrücken: **to reserve a table / to book a table**; **to reserve seats at the theatre / to book seats at the theatre**. Geläufiger ist jedoch **to book**, besonders in der Redewendung **to book a flight to ...** (einen Flug nach ... buchen).

➔ Merken Sie sich folgende Präpositionen:
to book a room AT your hotel;
I would be grateful FOR an indication of...;
AT your earliest convenience.

SIE SIND DRAN!

In diesem Abschnitt können Sie üben, die neuen Begriffe und Wendungen zu benutzen. Fällt Ihnen keine passende Lösung ein, dann schlagen Sie hier, wie in den folgenden Kapiteln, noch einmal im jeweiligen Teil „Redewendungen" nach. **Achtung**: Häufig sind mehrere Lösungen möglich und häufig steht eine Lücke für mehr als ein Wort!

> • I _____ to _____ a car _____ the month of May.
> I would be _____ if you could send me your daily _____ for
> a small four-seater car, and an indication _____ the current prices of
> petrol in Spain.

Lösung auf Seite 140

• *Vervollständigen Sie folgende Zeitungsannonce:*

> # FOR RENT
>
> beautiful villa on the island of Jersey.
> Four bedrooms, each _____ private
> bathroom; spacious lounge which _____
> the sea; swimming pool with diving board.

Lösung auf Seite 140

• *Beantworten Sie jetzt die Annonce:*

• Having seen your advertisement for the villa in Jersey, I _____ interested _____ from 1st – 30th September.
Please _____ at your earliest _____ whether this would be possible.

• I would like _____ a caravan _____ the weekend.
I _____ grateful if you _____ send some information on the different models available, as well as an _____ of your _____ rates.

• I am _____ to you in order to _____ a flight to Barbados _____ 10th July. I will be travelling with my wife and two children, and therefore will _____ four seats. We _____ to travel first class. I should be _____ if you would confirm the booking as _____ possible, as I must also make arrangements to _____ a car for our stay.

⌐━━⫞ Lösung auf Seite 140

LERNTIPPS

→ Notieren Sie nun die Wörter und Ausdrücke, die Ihnen besonders wichtig erscheinen. Welche waren Ihnen neu?

→ Auch wenn Sie nicht alles im Detail verstanden haben: Gehen Sie nach einiger Zeit zum nächsten Kapitel über, etwaige Unklarheiten lösen sich von selbst, wenn Sie etwas weiter sind.

2 TERMINE VEREINBAREN

GESCHÄFTLICHE TERMINE

Einer der wichtigsten Kunden von Luxiphon ist in Birmingham ansässig und Herr Müller möchte in dieser Firma die neuesten Telefonmodelle präsentieren. Er will deshalb mit Frau Angela Johnson, seiner Kontaktperson innerhalb dieser Firma, einen Termin ausmachen.

---

(1) _____

(2) _____ my letter of January 12th,
(3) _____ in Birmingham next week for the International
Telecommunications Fair. (4) _____ that
(5) _____ brought out a number of new models, and
I would have great pleasure in demonstrating them to you at some
point during the week. (6) _____ Tuesday 18th at
4 o'clock at your office?
(7) _____ convenient, you might like to propose an
alternative arrangement. (8) _____ this appointment as
soon as possible?
Should you have any further queries regarding our products,
(9) _____ .
I look forward to our next meeting.

Yours sincerely

Jens Müller

Jens Müller
Export Manager

⊶ Brief 2: Lösung auf Seite 132

Helfen Sie ihm, einen Geschäftstermin zu vereinbaren:

(1) *Die Anrede:*
Dear Sir / Madam
To whom it may concern
Dear Mrs Johnson

(2) *Sich auf einen vorausgegangenen Brief beziehen:*
As mentioned in
As told in
In view of

(3) *„Ich habe vor (am … in …) zu sein":*
I should be
I am planning to be
I hope to be

(4) *Die Aufmerksamkeit des Lesers erregen:*
You may be conscious
You may be interested to know
You must know

(5) *Welches Pronomen steht für die Firma?*
I have recently
we have recently
they have recently

(6) *Einen Vorschlag machen:*
May I suggest
How about
I propose

(7) *Eine negative Vermutung äußern:*
Should this not be
If this is not
In case this is not

(8) *Um eine Bestätigung bitten:*
Please confirm
You should confirm
Would you kindly confirm

(9) *„stehe ich Ihnen (gern) zur Verfügung":*
I remain at your disposal
I am available
please do not hesitate to contact me

PRIVATE TERMINE

Herr Müller erinnert sich, dass sein alter Freund George Grayson in Birmingham wohnt, und beschließt ihn auf seiner Reise zu besuchen. Er kündigt ihm seinen Besuch an und schlägt auch schon einen Termin vor.

Helfen Sie ihm, einen Brief mit einem Terminvorschlag vorzubereiten, und benutzen Sie jeweils einen der folgenden Begriffe. (Vergessen Sie dabei nicht, dass es sich um einen privaten Termin handelt!)

(1) _____

(2) _____ in Birmingham next week (3) _____,
and I was wondering if (4) _____ somewhere for dinner;
it seems such a long time since we last saw each other.
(5) _____ the White Horse Inn (6) _____ at 8?

Let me know during the week whether (7) _____ .
If you cannot make it maybe we can (8) _____ .

(9) _____ seeing you again!

(10) _____

Jens

Brief 3: Lösung auf Seite 132

(1) *Die Anrede:* Dear Mr Grayson Dear Sir Dear George	(5) *Etwas vorschlagen:* Maybe How about May I suggest
(2) *„Ich werde voraussichtlich sein":* I will I am due to be I am willing to be	(6) *Mit oder ohne Präposition?* Tuesday the Tuesday on Tuesday
(3) *„Geschäftlich":* on business for business to do business	(7) *Ob „es Ihnen / dir passt":* this is conventional this suits you this is comfortable for you
(4) *Welche ist die richtige Verbform?* we could meet we have met we would meet	(8) *Etwas anderes vereinbaren:* come to some other arrangement come to an agreement find something else

(9) *Der Schlusssatz:*
I am pleased to
Looking forward to
I hope to

(10) *Die Grußformel:*
Yours sincerely
Regards
With best wishes

 ## REDEWENDUNGEN

Sich auf einen vorausgegangenen, formellen Brief beziehen

As mentioned in my letter of… .

Wie in meinem Brief vom … erwähnt, … .

With reference to my letter of… .

Bezüglich meines Briefes vom … .

We refer to our letter of… .

Wir beziehen uns auf unseren Brief vom … .

Ein Projekt oder Vorhaben ankündigen

I am due to / I am to… .
I am planning to… .
I am likely to… .
I hope to… .
I intend to… .

Ich habe vor / Ich muss … .
Ich plane / Ich habe vor … zu … .
Wahrscheinlich werde ich … .
Ich hoffe / Ich habe vor … zu … .
Ich habe vor … zu … .

Auf etwas aufmerksam machen

You may be interested to know that… .

Vielleicht interessiert es Sie, dass … .

You may be aware that… .

Es wird Ihnen nicht entgangen sein, dass … .

It may have come to your attention that… .

Sie werden bemerkt haben, dass … .

We are pleased to inform you that… .

Wir freuen uns Ihnen mitteilen zu können, dass … .

Eine negative Vermutung äußern
formell:

Should this not be convenient (for you)… .

Sollte (Ihnen) das nicht möglich sein, … .

Should you be unavailable at this time… .

Sollten Sie zu diesem Zeitpunkt verhindert sein, … .

weniger formell:

If this is not convenient / suitable for you… .

Wenn Ihnen das nicht möglich ist, … .

If this does not suit you… .	*Wenn das Ihnen nicht gelegen ist, … .*
If this does not fit in with your plans / schedule… .	*Wenn es nicht in Ihren Zeitplan passt, … .*

Eine Dienstleistung anbieten

I would be pleased to… .	*Ich wäre erfreut, … .*
I would be grateful / glad for… .	*Ich wäre (Ihnen) dankbar für … .*
I would gladly… .	*Ich würde gern … .*

Um eine Bestätigung oder Antwort bitten
formell:

Would you kindly confirm / reply… ?	*Würden Sie bitte freundlicher-weise … bestätigen / beantworten?*
I would be obliged / grateful if you would confirm… .	*Ich wäre Ihnen sehr dankbar / verbunden, wenn Sie … bestäti-gen / beantworten könnten.*
Please confirm whether / if… .	*Bitte bestätigen Sie, ob … .*
Please inform me… .	*Bitte teilen Sie mir mit … .*

informell:

Let me know whether / if… .	*Lass / Lassen Sie mich wissen, ob …*
Tell me whether / if that is OK with you.	*Teil / Teilen Sie mir mit, ob das in Ordnung geht.*

Kontakte pflegen
formell:

Please do not hesitate to contact us should you have any further queries / require any further information.	*Sollten Sie weitere Fragen haben / weitere Informationen benötigen, zögern Sie nicht sich an uns zu wenden. Oder: Für weitere Auskünfte stehen wir Ihnen selbstverständlich jederzeit zur Verfügung.*
We look forward to hearing from you.	*Wir hoffen bald wieder von Ihnen zu hören.*

informell:

(I am) Looking forward to seeing you.	*Ich freue mich darauf dich / Sie zu sehen / zu treffen.*
I can't wait to see you.	*Ich kann es kaum erwarten dich zu sehen.*

 **ANMERKUNGEN**

➔ In den Sätzen **I am planning to be in Montreal next week** und **I am travelling to China next month** bezieht sich das Präsens auf eine Handlung in der Zukunft.

➔ Merken Sie sich die Präpositionen: **ON Tuesday, AT 4 o'clock.**

➔ Bis auf ganz wenige Ausnahmen, wie z. B. im Flugverkehr oder in militärischen Bereichen, wird die Uhrzeit im Englischen immer nur im 12-Stundenrhythmus angegeben. Um Missverständnisse auszuschließen, wird der Uhrzeit von 0 bis 12 Uhr ein **am** (Lateinisch für „ante meridiem" = vor dem Mittag), von 12.01 bis 23.59 Uhr ein **pm** (Lateinisch für „post meridiem" = nach dem Mittag) hinzugefügt. 12 Uhr ist **(12 o'clock) noon**, 24 Uhr heißt **(12 o'clock) midnight**.

➔ Beachten Sie den Bedeutungsunterschied zwischen den beiden abschließenden Sätzen:
I look forward to our next meeting. (In einem Geschäftsbrief = „sich freuen auf" plus Substantiv.)
(I am) LookING forward to seeING you again! (In einem persönlichen, emotionaleren Brief = „sich freuen auf" plus Verb plus -ING.)

➔ Unterscheiden Sie zwischen **if** und **whether**. Auch wenn sie oft die gleiche Bedeutung haben, so existiert doch in bestimmten Fällen ein feiner Unterschied: **whether** = ob (lässt eine Alternative offen), **if** = falls, ob (formuliert eine Bedingung).

➔ Beachten Sie auch, wie man sich auf das Datum eines Schreibens bezieht:
my letter of 12th January
my letter of January 12
my letter dated January 12th

SIE SIND DRAN!

Formelle Briefe:

* _____ reference _____ my letter _____ April 12th, I am _____ in London next week. I would like to _____ the opportunity to present our new catalogue. _____ I suggest 5th May _____ 3 pm? Should you be _____ on this date, you might like to propose an alternative arrangement.

* I _____ to travel to Kent _____ 15th March. The purpose of my trip _____ to visit our factory in the region. I hope to _____ pleasure _____ meeting you during my stay. I _____ suggest 17th March _____ 5 o'clock at your office. _____ confirm if you _____ available at this time.

Lösung auf Seite 140

Informelle Briefe:

* I am _____ to be in Somerset in June _____ the Flower Festival. I was _____ if we could meet somewhere _____ lunch. _____ the Bull Inn on Friday _____ 2 pm?

* I _____ to be travelling to Dhaka next Monday. _____ if we could meet there _____ the evening. I would _____ the Hilton Hotel _____ 7 pm in the lobby.

* Sie möchten demnächst nach London fliegen. Informieren Sie Ihren Freund William über Ihre bevorstehende Reise. Teilen Sie ihm mit, dass Sie ihn gerne am Montag, dem 8. März um 21 Uhr vor „Victoria Station" treffen würden, um gemeinsam etwas trinken zu gehen.

Lösung auf Seite 140

3 RESERVIERUNGEN BESTÄTIGEN

Herr Müller erhält vom Hotel die Bestätigung seiner Zimmerreservierung.

---

(1) _____

(2) _____ of 4th February (3) _____ a single room
with bath and shower and a view of the gardens.

(4) _____ the accommodation you describe
(5) _____ you require, and (6) _____ if you
would (7) _____ of £20 as soon as possible
(8) _____ the reservation.

We (9) _____ your stay with us.

(10) _____

Marion Hunter

Marion Hunter
Reservations Manager

Brief 4: Lösung auf Seite 132

Rekonstruieren Sie den Antwortbrief des Hotels mit Hilfe folgender Elemente:

(1) *Die Anrede:*
Dear Jens
Dear Mr Müller
Dear Sir / Madam

(2) *Den Erhalt des Briefes bestätigen:*
Thank you for your letter
Thanks a lot for your letter
We are in reception of your letter

(3) *An den Inhalt des Briefes erinnern:*
requesting us to book
demanding a booking for
asking for a reservation for

(4) *Welche ist die richtige Verbform?*
I have reserved
I would have reserved
I am reserving

(5) *Welche ist die korrekte Präposition?*
for the period
on the period
at the period

(6) *Ich „wäre Ihnen dankbar":*
should be grateful
should recognise you
should be pleased

(7) *Eine Anzahlung leisten:*
forward a deposit
send a guarantee
enclose a fine

(8) *(Die Reservierung) bestätigen:*
to confine
to restrict
to confirm

(9) *„(Wir) freuen (uns) auf":*
look forward to
can't wait to
look after

(10) *Die Grußformel:*
Yours faithfully
Yours sincerely
Best regards

Dear Mr Müller

Thank you for your letter of 4th February requesting us to book a single room with bath and shower and a view of the gardens.

Unfortunately (1) _____ for the period you require because of the International Telecommunications Fair. However, (2) _____ an alternative hotel, also a member of the Palace chain of hotels. Although (3) _____ of being located on the outskirts of the city, (4) _____ you will find the hotel (5) _____ and its surroundings most pleasant. The address is:
Regency Hotel, 182 Brompton Road, Birmingham.

We remain (6) _____ for any future reservations you might wish to make.

Yours sincerely

Marion Hunter

Marion Hunter
Reservations Manager

Brief 5: Lösung auf Seite 132

Im Falle eines negativen Bescheids vom Hotel wird der erste Absatz, in dem auf die Anfrage Bezug genommen wird, wahrscheinlich identisch sein. Vervollständigen Sie den zweiten Teil des Briefes mit Hilfe folgender Begriffe:

(1) *Mitteilen, dass das Hotel belegt ist:*
we are overbooked
we are fully booked
we are full

(2) *Einen Vorschlag machen:*
we may suggest
we are able to recommend
we propose

(3) *Eine kleine Unannehmlichkeit*
mitteilen:
it is a disadvantage
it has the serious problem
it has the slight inconvenience

(4) *Sich einer Sache sicher sein:*
no doubt
I am confident
I am certain

(5) *Den Kunden zufriedenstellen:*
to your total satisfaction
quite satisfactory
not bad

(6) *„Zu Ihrer Verfügung":*
at your disposition
at your convenience
at your service

 # REDEWENDUNGEN

Den Eingang eines Briefes bestätigen

Thank you for your letter of… in which you request us to… .
In reply to your letter of… .
With reference to your enquiry of… .

Vielen Dank für Ihren Brief vom …, in dem Sie uns bitten, … zu … .
Als Antwort auf Ihren Brief vom … .
Bezüglich Ihrer Anfrage vom … .

Eine Reservierung bestätigen

We are writing to confirm your telephone call this morning in which you requested us to book two business class seats on the next flight to Tokyo. Enclosed are the tickets and invoice.
This is to confirm our telephone conversation of… in which I booked a double room and two single rooms for four nights in the name of Mr. Hamilton. Enclosed is a cheque for £20 to cover the deposit.

Hiermit bestätigen wir Ihren Anruf von heute morgen, in dem Sie uns baten, zwei Business-Class-Plätze für den nächsten Flug nach Tokyo zu buchen. Flugtickets und Rechnung liegen bei.
Hiermit bestätige ich unser Telefonat vom …, in dem ich ein Doppel- und zwei Einzelzimmer für 4 Nächte auf den Namen Hamilton bestellt habe. Beiliegend ein Scheck über £20 als Anzahlung.

I have reserved the accommodation you describe for the week 5th – 12th January.

We are writing to confirm availability of an estate car for the period 4th – 25th August. Please find enclosed our current rates and conditions of hire.

We are pleased to confirm your reservation of a holiday villa from 1st – 30th June inclusive. We enclose a short description of how to reach the holiday complex.

Ich habe die von Ihnen benannte Unterkunft für die Woche vom 5. bis 12. Januar gebucht.

Hiermit bestätigen wir, dass für die Zeit vom 4. bis 25. August ein Kombiwagen verfügbar ist. Beiliegend finden Sie unsere aktuellen Tarife und Mietbedingungen.

Wir freuen uns, Ihre Reservierung einer Ferienvilla vom 1. bis 30. Juni bestätigen zu können. Wir fügen eine kurze Wegbeschreibung zu unserer Ferienanlage bei.

Eine Reservierung ablehnen

We regret to inform you that we are fully booked throughout the month of May.

Unfortunately there are no seats left for Saturday evening's performance of "The Tempest".

I am afraid there are no more places available for next weekend's trip to Amsterdam.

We regret to inform you that we have no estate cars available for the weekend of 4th – 7th July.

Wir bedauern Ihnen mitteilen zu müssen, dass wir im gesamten Monat Mai ausgebucht sind.

Leider gibt es am Samstag für die Abendaufführung von „The Tempest" keine Karten mehr.

Leider sind für die Reise nach Amsterdam am kommenden Wochenende keine Plätze mehr frei.

Wir bedauern Ihnen mitteilen zu müssen, dass wir für das Wochenende vom 4. bis 7. Juli keine Kombiwagen mehr zur Verfügung haben.

Eine Alternative vorschlagen

May I suggest you contact the Sunrise Hotel (address below) who may be able to offer you suitable accommodation for the period you require?

We can, however, offer you five seats for the matinee on Saturday.

May I suggest that in future you book at least one month in advance, as this is a very popular excursion?

We suggest you contact one of the other branches in the area who may be able to help you.

Ich schlage Ihnen vor, sich an das Sunrise Hotel zu wenden (Adresse s. u.), das Ihnen vielleicht eine adäquate Unterkunft für die gewünschte Zeit anbieten kann.

Wir können Ihnen jedoch fünf Plätze für die Nachmittagsvorstellung am Samstag anbieten.

Ich rate Ihnen, künftig mindestens einen Monat im Voraus zu buchen, da diese Rundfahrt sehr beliebt ist.

Wir schlagen Ihnen vor, sich an eine andere Agentur in der Gegend zu wenden, die Ihnen möglicherweise weiterhelfen kann.

ANMERKUNGEN

→ Das Hotel hätte auch einfach mit dem Satz **We are writing to confirm** antworten können: **Thank you for your letter of… . We are writing to confirm your reservation of a single room… .**

→ Beachten Sie, dass zwischen **week** und dem Datum kein „of" steht.

→ Vorsicht: Man sagt a **view OF** für „mit Blick auf", aber **a room with A view** für „ein Zimmer mit Aussicht".

 **SIE SIND DRAN !**

• We _____ to inform you _____ there are no bicycles _____ for the period you require. We _____ you contact the Cambridge Bicycle Centre. They _____ to help you.

• I am writing _____ your reservation _____ three first class seats on Friday's flight _____ Bangkok, arriving on 30th July. Please find enclosed your tickets and our invoice.

• _____ for your letter of 7th May. We are _____ to confirm your reservation _____ a yacht _____ 4th June - 3rd July. Enclosed are our charges and our conditions of hire.

• With reference to _____ telephone conversation of 13th April, we are pleased _____ your reservation _____ package tour to India _____ two people.

Lösung auf Seite 140 / 141

4 TERMINE BESTÄTIGEN

EINEN TERMINVORSCHLAG ANNEHMEN

Die beiden Personen, mit denen sich Herr Müller während seines Aufenthaltes in Birmingham treffen möchte, können den Termin wahrnehmen.

ELECTRON Ltd. **25 St James Street Birmingham B25 8HO**

Mr J Müller
Luxiphon
Magdeburger Str. 250
10785 Berlin   13th February 19...

Your ref: JM / RJ
Our ref: AJ / PW

1) _____

(2) _____ for your letter of 10th February.
(3) _____ that I (4) _____ to see you
(5) _____ on Tuesday 18th (6) _____ .

(7) _____

Angela Johnson

Angela Johnson

Brief 6: Lösung auf Seite 133

Rekonstruieren Sie Frau Johnsons Zusage mit Hilfe folgender Redewendungen:

(1) *Die Anrede:*
  Dear Mr Müller
  Dear Sir / Madam
  Dear Jens

(2) *Sich bedanken:*
  Thanks a lot
  Thank you
  I am most grateful

(3) *Bestätigen:*
I would like to confirm
I agree
I give confirmation

(4) *Zur Verfügung stehen:*
will be available
am ready
will be disposable

(5) *Welche Präposition ist richtig?*
on my office
at my office
in my office

(6) *Die Uhrzeit bestätigen:*
at the hour you suggest
any time you like
at the time you propose

(7) *Die Grußformel:*
Yours sincerely
Regards
Yours faithfully

EINEN TERMIN VERSCHIEBEN

Wie würde Frau Johnson das Schreiben formulieren, falls sie den Termin absagen müsste?

Dear Mr Müller

With reference to your letter of 10th February, (1) _____
to inform you that (2) _____ to meet you on Tuesday
18th February (3) _____ a company meeting. However,
(4) _____ we (5) _____ to the following day
(6) _____ ?

I look forward to (7) _____ .

Yours sincerely

Angela Johnson

Angela Johnson

⚬━━▌ Brief 7: Lösung auf Seite 133

(1) *Bedauern ausdrücken:*
   I am regretful
   I regret
   sorry

(2) *Nicht zur Verfügung stehen:*
   I shall not be disposed
   I shall not be available
   I shall not be disposable

(3) *„Wegen":*
   owing to
   owing at
   owed of

(4) *Einen Vorschlag machen:*
   it is my suggestion
   may I suggest
   it is suggested

(5) *Einen Termin verschieben:*
   adjourn the meeting
   postpone the appointment
   put off the interview

(6) *Welche Präposition ist richtig?*
   on the same time
   at the same time
   in the same time

(7) *Umgehende Antwort erhalten:*
   receiving an early confirmation
   receiving a reply quickly
   your rapid response

Vergleichen Sie Frau Johnsons Antwort mit der von George, die in einem ganz anderen Stil gehalten ist:

Dear Jens

Thanks a lot for your letter. It would be lovely to see you when you come over to Birmingham next week. The White Horse Inn sounds an excellent idea. Tuesday at 8 is fine by me. I've invited some friends to come along too.

Best wishes

George

REDEWENDUNGEN

Sich auf einen vorausgegangenen Brief beziehen

informell:

Thanks a lot for your letter.	*Danke für deinen Brief.*

formell:

Thank you for your letter of… .	*Vielen Dank für Ihren Brief vom …*
With reference to your letter of… .	*Wir beziehen uns auf Ihren Brief vom … .*

Einen Termin bestätigen

informell:

It would be lovely to see you.	*Es wäre schön dich (wieder)zusehen.*
That sounds an excellent idea.	*Das klingt gut / Das ist eine gute Idee.*
Monday at 3 is fine by me.	*Montag um 3 (Uhr) passt mir.*

formell:

I would like to confirm (that I will be available to see you / have dinner with you / meet you).	*Ich möchte hiermit bestätigen, (dass ich für einen Termin mit Ihnen / für ein Abendessen mit Ihnen / für ein Treffen mit Ihnen zur Verfügung stehe).*
I should like to confirm our meeting / our appointment.	*Ich möchte unser Treffen / unseren Termin (hiermit) bestätigen.*
This is to confirm the appointment we made on… .	*Hiermit bestätige ich den Termin, den wir am … festgelegt hatten.*

Einen Termin absagen / verlegen

informell:

I'm afraid I won't be able to come, as I have something else on.	*Leider werde ich nicht kommen können, da ich etwas anderes vorhabe.*
Sorry, but I am busy on that day. How about the week after?	*Tut mir leid, aber an dem Tag habe ich keine Zeit. Wie wär's denn die Woche darauf?*

formell:

I regret to inform you that… .	*Ich bedaure Ihnen mitteilen zu müssen, dass … .*
I am unavailable on that day; I suggest we postpone the meeting to the following week.	*An dem (fraglichen) Tag habe ich keine Zeit. Ich schlage vor, das Treffen auf die darauf folgende Woche zu verlegen.*

I am afraid that I am obliged to change the date of our meeting, due to a problem with… .

Unfortunately, I will be out of the country for two weeks; may I suggest I get in touch with you on my return to arrange another appointment?

I wonder if I might ask you to postpone the meeting to 4 o'clock on the same afternoon.

I apologize for the inconvenience.

Leider bin ich wegen eines Problems mit … gezwungen, den Termin unseres Treffens zu verlegen.

Leider werde ich für zwei Wochen außer Landes sein und möchte deshalb vorschlagen, dass ich mich nach meiner Rückkehr wegen eines neuen Termins bei Ihnen melde.

Dürfte ich Sie bitten, das Treffen auf 4 Uhr am selben Nachmittag zu verlegen?

Für etwaige Ungelegenheiten möchte ich mich entschuldigen.

Einen Termin absagen
informell:

I'm afraid I won't be able to make it after all.

Sorry, but I will have to cancel lunch on Thursday as I have an important meeting.

Ich fürchte, ich werde es doch nicht schaffen.

(Es) Tut mir leid, aber wegen eines wichtigen Termins muss ich das Mittagessen am Donnerstag absagen.

formell:

Much to my regret, I am forced to cancel our forthcoming meeting owing to a problem which has arisen in our Leipzig office.

I am afraid I will not be able to keep the appointment I made for Tuesday 5th January, owing to… .

I apologize for the inconvenience this must cause you.

Zu meinem (größten) Bedauern bin ich gezwungen, unser geplantes Treffen abzusagen, da in unserem Leipziger Büro ein Problem aufgetaucht ist.

Leider werde ich wegen … nicht in der Lage sein den Termin einzuhalten, den ich für Dienstag, den 5. Januar vereinbart habe.

Ich entschuldige mich für die Unannehmlichkeiten, die Ihnen hierdurch entstehen.

ANMERKUNGEN

→ Beachten Sie den Gebrauch des Präsens, um über eine Handlung in der Zukunft zu sprechen: **I am unavailable on that day**.

→ Eine Begründung muss nicht immer mit **BECAUSE** formuliert werden; einfacher ist es oft, **OWING TO** + Substantiv oder **AS** + Aussagesatz zu benutzen:
owing to a meeting = wegen eines Termins
as I have a meeting = da ich einen Termin habe

→ Merken Sie sich die Präpositionen in folgenden Redewendungen:
Tuesday is fine BY me: Dienstag passt mir
Much TO my regret: Zu meinem (größten) Bedauern

SIE SIND DRAN!

• I am _____ I won't be able to make it _____ the theatre on Friday as I have _____ on.

• With reference to your letter _____ 6th March,
I _____ to confirm that I shall be _____ to meet you _____ 20th May to discuss a possible partnership.

• Much _____ I am obliged to cancel our _____ meeting, _____ a sudden illness. I _____ for any _____ caused, and I shall contact you as soon as possible to _____ another meeting.

• In reply to your letter _____ 20th January, I should _____ pleased to meet you _____ Friday, but _____ prefer it if the meeting could be postponed to take place later in the afternoon.

• *Sie schreiben einem Freund, um das für kommenden Donnerstag geplante Frühstück abzusagen, da Sie auf eine Geschäftsreise gehen müssen. Sie entschuldigen sich und schlagen vor, das Frühstück auf den darauf folgenden Dienstag zu verlegen.*

Lösung auf Seite 141

5 INFORMATIONEN EINHOLEN

UNTERLAGEN ANFORDERN

Die Internationale Messe für Telekommunikation brachte hervorragende Ergebnisse. Herr Müller bekommt zahlreiche Anfragen von interessierten Kunden, die Unterlagen und genauere Angaben zu Luxiphon-Produkten anfordern.

MATTHEWS & SONS   7 Banbury Avenue
Sydney · Australia

The Export Manager
Luxiphon
Magdeburger Str. 250
10785 Berlin
Germany   2nd March 19…

Ref: HP / RW

(1) _____

(2) _____ your stand at the International Telecommunications Fair in Birmingham, (3) _____ that you
produce some very innovative designs of luxury telephones.
(4) _____ quality electrical and office machinery, and feel
(5) _____ here for your type of product.
(6) _____ further details of your '20s style and pyramidal
models, (7) _____ (8) _____ of your current
catalogue showing prices and colour ranges if possible?
(9) _____ an early reply.

Yours faithfully

Harold Percy
Harold Percy
General Manager

Brief 8: Lösung auf Seite 133

Rekonstruieren Sie den Brief eines Interessenten mit Hilfe nachstehender Ausdrücke:

(1) *Die Anrede:*
Dear Sir
Dear Jens
Dear Mr Müller

(2) *Welche ist die richtige Verbform?*
Having recently visited
I was recently visiting
I will visit

(3) *Interesse zeigen:*
I was amazed
I was interested to see
I was delighted to know

(4) *Die Firma und ihre Produkte vorstellen:*
We are importers of
We are a supplier of
I am a supply company of

(5) *Einen expandierenden Markt beschreiben:*
there are good facilities
there is a promising market
there is plenty of demand

(6) *Etwas anfordern:*
We want
Could you please send
Thank you for sending

(7) *„Sowohl … als auch":*
as well as
and
and also

(8) *„Ein Exemplar" (eines Katalogs):*
an example
a selection
a copy

(9) *„Wir freuen uns auf / In Erwartung":*
Thank you for
We hope for
We look forward to

SONDERWÜNSCHE ÄUSSERN

Herr Müller erhält auch einen ungewöhnlichen Brief: ein arabischer Scheich möchte wissen, ob Luxiphon goldene Telefone herstellt und ob es darüber hinaus möglich ist, den Hörer mit Brillanten zu besetzen …

Dear Sir

(1) _____ the International Telecommunications Fair in
Birmingham, (2) _____ your company's original designs
and variety of models.

(3) _____ a gold-coloured version of model number 36.
(4) _____ , (5) _____ it would be
possible for your company to manufacture them with several small diamonds
inlaid in the receiver.

(6) _____ , please inform my secretary at the above
address as soon as possible, so that we can proceed with the appropriate
arrangements.

Yours faithfully

Sheik Malik

Sheik Malik

○━━▪ Brief 9: Lösung auf Seite 133

Vervollständigen Sie mit Hilfe folgender Elemente den Brief des Scheichs:

(1) *Sich auf einen vorhergehenden*
   Kontakt beziehen:
   We met at
   While recently visiting your
      stand at
   Having talked to you at

(2) *Interesse zeigen:*
   I was overwhelmed by
   I was very impressed with
   I liked the green model best of

(3) *Sich nach einem Produkt er-*
   kundigen:
   Do you do
   I would like information on
   I would be interested to know
      whether you produce

(4) *„Darüber hinaus":*
   Furthermore
   However
   On the other hand

(5) *Eine Auskunft einholen:*
   I wanted to enquire whether
   I want to know whether
   I want to know if

(6) *„Sollten Sie unseren Wünschen*
   nachkommen können":
   If you can do what I want
   Should you be able to satisfy
      these requirements
   If this is OK by you

 **REDEWENDUNGEN**

Auf erste Kontakte oder Werbeanzeigen Bezug nehmen

While recently visiting… .	*Während ich vor kurzem … besuchte, … .*
Having recently attended… .	*Da ich kürzlich an … teilgenommen habe, … .*
	Nachdem ich kürzlich an … teilgenommen hatte, … .
I recently visited… .	*Kürzlich besuchte ich … .*
After having visited… .	*Nachdem ich … besucht hatte, … .*
I am writing to ask for details on… as advertised in "The Times" on Tuesday 26th August.	*Bitte schicken Sie mir detaillierte Angaben über …, wie in Ihrer Anzeige in „The Times" vom Dienstag, dem 26. August beschrieben.*
I was given your name by Mr… .	*Herr … nannte mir Ihren Namen.*

Interesse an etwas Bestimmtem äußern

I was very impressed with… .	*Ich war sehr beeindruckt von … .*
I greatly admire… .	*Ich bewundere … sehr.*
I was interested to see / hear / know that… .	*Es interessierte mich zu sehen / hören / erfahren, dass … .*
We are interested in… .	*Wir sind an … interessiert.*
We are looking for potential suppliers of… .	*Wir suchen nach möglichen / potenziellen Lieferanten für … .*

Einen potenziellen Markt aufzeigen

There are good opportunities for this product.	*Dieses Produkt hat gute Perspektiven.*
There is a promising market for… .	*Für … existiert ein vielversprechender Markt.*
There is a good potential for… .	*… ist sehr entwicklungsfähig.*
There is much demand for… .	*Es herrscht große Nachfrage nach … .*
There is a brisk trade in… .	*(Auf dem Gebiet von) … existiert ein lebhafter Handel.*
More and more of our regular customers are showing an interest in this type of product.	*Eine ständig wachsende Zahl unserer Stammkunden zeigt ihr Interesse an diesem Produkt(typ).*

Unterlagen, Informationen usw. anfordern

Could you please send… ?	*Könnten Sie (uns) bitte … schicken?*
Would you kindly send… ?	*Würden Sie (uns) freundlicherweise … schicken?*
We would be grateful for… .	*Wir wären für … dankbar.*
We would like… .	*Wir hätten gern … .*

some information about / on / of...	*Informationen über ...*
a quotation for...	*einen Kostenvoranschlag über ...*
some documentation on...	*Unterlagen über ...*
further details about / on / of...	*weitere Informationen über ...*
samples of...	*Muster / Proben von ... (oder:*
	-muster / -proben)
prices for...	*die Preise für ...*

Auskünfte einholen

Could you tell me if... ?	*Könnten Sie mir sagen, ob ... ?*
I would like to inquire if / whether... .	*Ich möchte nachfragen, ob ... .*
I would be interested to know whether... or... .	*Ich wüsste gern, ob ... oder ... .*

Den Inhalt der Unterlagen genau angeben

a catalogue	*ein Katalog*
a leaflet	*eine Broschüre*
a quotation	*ein Kostenvoranschlag*
an estimate	*eine Schätzung*
with prices	*mit Preisen*
including pictures and samples	*mit Abbildungen und Mustern*
showing prices and colour ranges	*mit Preisen und Farbskalen*
with an indication of prices	*mit Preisangabe*

Fracht- und Versicherungskosten erfragen

Please let us know the current freight rate for air / sea / rail / road transport.	*Bitte nennen Sie uns die derzeitigen Kosten für Luft- / See- / Schienen- / Straßenfracht.*
We should be grateful if you would quote us your lowest rate for the despatch of... from Berlin to New York by air.	*Wir wären dankbar, wenn Sie uns Ihre niedrigsten Luftfrachtkosten für ... von Berlin nach New York nennen könnten.*
Could you please quote charges for shipment and insurance of a consignment of books measuring 2 m by 1 m and weighing 200 kilos?	*Könnten Sie uns bitte die Kosten für Verschiffung / Transport und Versicherung einer Büchersendung mit den Maßen 2 x 1 m und einem Gewicht von 200 kg geben?*

Zusätzlich um etwas bitten

Furthermore, I would like... .	*Darüber hinaus hätte ich gern ... .*
In addition I would like... .	*Zusätzlich hätte ich gern ... .*
I would also like... .	*Ich hätte außerdem gern ... .*
Besides the telephones, I would like... .	*Außer den Telefonen hätte ich gern ... .*

as well as a catalogue…	*neben einem Katalog …*
together with…	*zusammen mit …*
in addition to…	*zusätzlich zu …*

Nach Zusatzleistungen fragen

I wanted to enquire whether your company could… .	*Ich hätte (gern) gewusst, ob Ihre Firma … könnte.*
Would it be possible for your company to… ?	*Wäre es Ihrer Firma möglich, … ?*
Could / Would your company be able to… ?	*Könnte / Wäre Ihre Firma in der Lage … ?*

Anforderungen oder Wünschen entsprechen

satisfy these requirements	*diesen Anforderungen entsprechen*
fulfil these requirements	*diese Anforderungen erfüllen*
cater to my needs	*meine Bedürfnisse befriedigen*

Um eine Antwort bitten

Please inform my secretary… .	*Bitte informieren Sie meine Sekretärin … .*
Please get in touch with… .	*Bitte nehmen Sie mit … Kontakt auf.*
Please contact… .	*Bitte kontaktieren Sie … .*
We look forward to an early reply.	*Wir freuen uns auf Ihre baldige Antwort.*
We look forward to receiving your catalogue / quotation as soon as possible.	*Wir freuen uns auf die schnellstmögliche Zusendung Ihres Katalogs / Kostenvoranschlags.*
Please reply as soon as possible / without delay.	*Bitte antworten Sie so schnell wie möglich / umgehend.*
Please send your reply to… .	*Bitte senden Sie Ihr Antwortschreiben an … .*
Please reply by return of post.	*Bitte antworten Sie möglichst umgehend.*

Schlussformeln

Please do not hesitate to contact us.	*Bitte zögern Sie nicht sich mit uns in Verbindung zu setzen.*
Please do not hesitate to let us know if we can be of any further help.	*Bitte zögern Sie nicht uns mitzuteilen, ob wir Ihnen weiterhelfen können.*
We thank you in advance for any information you can provide.	*Wir danken Ihnen im Voraus für alle Informationen, die Sie uns zur Verfügung stellen können.*

ANMERKUNGEN

→ Beachten Sie: **SHOULD you be able to satisfy...** (sollten Sie in der Lage sein, ... zu erfüllen) ist bei weitem höflicher als „IF you ARE able to satisfy" (wenn Sie ... erfüllen können).

→ Beachten Sie folgende Präpositionen:
to be impressed WITH: beeindruckt sein von
to place an order FOR: eine Bestellung / einen Auftrag erteilen für / über
AS well AS: sowohl ... als auch
in addition TO: zusätzlich zu

→ **Besides** (neben / außer) wird ohne Präposition und am Satzanfang benutzt: **Besides the catalogue, I would like a number of samples**.

SIE SIND DRAN !

> • While _____ your factory, _____ very impressed with your manufacturing procedures. _____ be interested to know _____ you produce smaller sizes of model number 2. I would like to _____ 500 pairs _____ sunglasses, model no. 546. _____ satisfy these requirements, please _____ secretary at the _____ address.
>
> • Having _____ your stand _____ the trade fair, I would _____ details about your telephones, model no. 99. Please _____ me _____ my office under this number.
>
> • We are wholesalers in the tea trade, and we _____ some information _____ the types of tea you produce. Would you _____ send _____ your latest catalogue _____ prices, as well as a selection of samples?

• *Die folgende Annonce weckt Ihr Interesse. Fordern Sie Unterlagen und Muster an:*
WE MANUFACTURE EXQUISITE COUNTRY PERFUMES MADE EXCLUSIVELY FROM NATURAL INGREDIENTS. CONTACT US FOR A FREE CATALOGUE AND SAMPLES.

Lösung auf Seite 141

6 BESTELLUNGEN AUFGEBEN

Einige Kunden geben Bestellungen für besondere Telefonmodelle auf, nachdem sie von Herrn Müller Kostenvoranschläge erhalten haben.

TELEWARES   55 HAMPTON ROAD • GUILDFORD • SURREY PQ55 6TO

Mr J Müller
Export Department
Luxiphon
Magdeburger Str. 250
10785 Berlin   6th March 19…

(1) _____

(2) _____ of March 1st. We have pleasure in
(3) _____ with you for the following:

QUANTITY	NAME	MODEL	COLOUR	PRICE
50	Mars	M. 234	Green	£25.56
25	Princess	P.52	Pink	£30.05
70	Duo	D.07	Turquoise	£22.90

(4) _____ this order by returning the duplicate to us,
(5) _____ .

(6) _____

P. Cunningham

P Cunningham
Buyer

✂ Brief 10: Lösung auf Seite 133 / 134

Vervollständigen Sie mit Hilfe folgender Begriffe die Bestellung:

(1) *Die Anrede:*
Dear Jens
Dear Sir / Madam
Dear Mr Müller

(2) *Den Erhalt des Kostenvoran-
schlags bestätigen:*
Thanks a lot for your quotation
Thank you for your quotation
Thankfully, we received your
quotation

(3) *„Eine Bestellung aufgeben":*
giving an order
placing an order
ordering

(4) *Um eine Auftragsbestätigung bitten:*
Please acknowledge
We would be grateful for your
acknowledgement
You will have acknowledged

(5) *„ordnungsgemäß unterzeichnet":*
as signed
to be signed
duly signed

(6) *Die Grußformel:*
Yours sincerely
With best wishes
Yours faithfully

 REDEWENDUNGEN

Den Eingang bestätigen

Thank you for your letter / your
quotation of… .
With reference to your letter / quotation of… .

*Vielen Dank für Ihren Brief / Kosten-
voranschlag vom … .*
*Wir beziehen uns auf Ihren Brief /
Kostenvoranschlag vom … .*

Eine Bestellung aufgeben / ordern

to order
to place an order
We are pleased to place an order
with you for… .
Please send us the undermentioned
goods.
Please supply us with… .

We would like to place an order
for… .
With reference to your quotation,
we enclose our order for… .

bestellen, ordern
eine Bestellung aufgeben
*Wir möchten bei Ihnen gern eine
Bestellung über … aufgeben.*
*Bitte schicken / senden Sie uns die
unten genannten Waren.*
*Bitte schicken Sie uns / beliefern
Sie uns mit … .*

*Wir möchten eine Bestellung für /
über … aufgeben.*
*Wir beziehen uns auf Ihren Kosten-
voranschlag und fügen unsere
Bestellung über … bei.*

Den Liefertermin genau nennen

We should be grateful for delivery by… (date).

Please confirm that you can supply these goods by the required date.

We enclose our order for immediate delivery.

Für eine Lieferung bis zum … (Datum) wären wir dankbar.

Bitte bestätigen Sie, dass Sie die Waren bis zum gewünschten Termin liefern können.

Wir fügen unsere Bestellung bei und bitten um umgehende Lieferung.

Der Bestellschein / Das Bestellformular

order number / order no.

Please write in block letters.

Please send this order form together with your remittance to… .

A copy of the invoice should be included in the package.

Please quote the number on all correspondence.

Bestellnummer / Bestell-Nr.

Bitte in Blockschrift schreiben.

Bitte schicken Sie diesen Bestellschein zusammen mit Ihrer Überweisung an … .

Eine Rechnungskopie sollte dem Paket beiliegen.

Bitte geben Sie die Nummer in allen Ihren Schreiben an.

Um eine Auftragsbestätigung bitten

Please acknowledge this order by return of post.

Please confirm receipt of this order.

Please sign the duplicate of this order and return it to us as an acknowledgement.

Bitte bestätigen Sie diesen Auftrag möglichst umgehend.

Bitte bestätigen Sie den Erhalt dieser Bestellung.

Bitte unterschreiben Sie das Doppel dieser Bestellung und schicken Sie es uns als Bestätigung zurück.

Ein Angebot ablehnen

The samples sent lead us to believe your products are not of the standard we require.

We feel that your products do not meet our requirements and we shall therefore not be placing an order for them.

I am afraid your products do not have the technical specifications required for sale in this country.

I am afraid your prices are not competitive enough. We have therefore decided not to place an order with you.

Die zugeschickten Muster lassen uns annehmen, dass Ihre Produkte nicht dem Standard entsprechen, den wir erwarten.

Wir glauben, dass Ihre Produkte nicht den (gängigen) Anforderungen entsprechen und werden deshalb von einer Bestellung absehen.

Ich fürchte, Ihre Produkte weisen nicht die technische Qualität auf, die bei einem Verkauf in diesem Land gefordert wird.

Ich fürchte, Ihre Preise sind nicht wettbewerbsfähig / konkurrenzfähig. Wir werden deshalb von einer Bestellung absehen.

An eine fällige Lieferung erinnern

Re our order no. ... .

We wish to remind you that our order no. ... has not yet been delivered.

As we have not yet received... .

Please inform us by return of post as to the expected date of delivery.

Please give this matter your immediate attention.

Bezüglich unserer Bestellung Nr. ... .

Wir möchten (Sie) daran erinnern, dass unsere Bestellung Nr. ... noch nicht geliefert wurde.

Da wir ... noch nicht erhalten haben, ...

Bitte teilen Sie uns umgehend den voraussichtlichen Liefertermin mit.

Bitte erledigen Sie diese Angelegenheit umgehend.

Eine Bestellung abändern oder stornieren

Should any items be out of stock, please submit a quotation for a substitute.

We should like to cancel our order no. ... owing to... .

Sollten einzelne Teile nicht auf Lager sein, schicken Sie bitte einen Kostenvoranschlag für einen vergleichbaren Artikel.

Wir möchten unsere Bestellung Nr. ... stornieren, weil ... .

 ANMERKUNGEN

→ Beachten Sie den Gebrauch der verschiedenen Präpositionen: **thank you FOR / your quotation OF** (+ Datum) / **we have pleasure IN**.

→ Verben, die auf die Präpositionen **IN** und **BY** folgen, hängen die Endung **-ing** an: **pleasure IN placING, acknowledge BY returnING**...

→ Vergessen Sie nicht, dass „eine Bestellung BEI jemandem aufgeben" im Englischen so ausgedrückt wird: **to place an order WITH someone**.

 **SIE SIND DRAN!**

- I _____ two large turkeys for Christmas Day. _____ this order by return of post.

- _____ your quotation _____ 6th November. We _____ pleasure _____ an order _____ you for the _____ items. Please _____ that you can supply the goods _____ the end of the month.

- Thank you _____ your quotation. We feel however that your _____ do not meet our _____ . We shall therefore not _____ an order with you.

- We have pleasure in placing _____ 500 Garard hi-fis and 200 Blaster portable radios for _____ delivery. Please sign the _____ of this order and return it to us as an acknowledgement.

- *Geben Sie eine Bestellung über 20 Paar Schuhe Modell „Aschenputtel" (Cinderella), Größe 36 (5) auf. Bitten Sie um eine umgehende Lieferung.*

⚷ Lösung auf Seite 141 / 142

7 BESTELLUNGEN BEANTWORTEN

EINEN AUFTRAG BESTÄTIGEN

Herr Müller schreibt mehrere Auftragsbestätigungen. Meistens bestätigt er, dass die Bestellung zum vereinbarten Termin ausgeführt werden kann. Manchmal muss er dem Kunden jedoch mitteilen, dass ein Modell nicht vorrätig ist.

Mr P Cunningham
Telewares
55 Hampton Road
Guildford
Surrey PQ66 5ST   11th March 19...

(1) _____

Thank you for (2) _____ 6th March. (3) _____ ,
(4) _____ the duplicate (5) _____ in acknowledgement of your order. Our dispatch department
(6) _____ your order and will inform you when
(7) _____ is (8) _____ .

(9) _____ for your custom and (10) _____
being of service to you again in the near future.

Yours sincerely

J. Müller

J Müller
Export Manager

Brief 11: Lösung auf Seite 134

Gestalten Sie mit Hilfe folgender Elemente eine Auftragsbestätigung:

(1) *Die Anrede:*
To whom it may concern
Dear Sir
Dear Mr Cunningham

(2) *„Ihre Bestellung / Ihr Auftrag*
Nr. ... vom":
your command no. 67 of
your order no. 67 dated
your demand no. 67 from

(3) *„wie gewünscht":*
As you ask
As requested
As you wish

(4) *„wir fügen bei":*
we include
we add
we enclose

(5) *„ordnungsgemäß unterzeichnet":*
correctly signed
duly signed
signed as required

(6) *Die Versandabteilung*
„bearbeitet nun":
is currently processing
is responsible for
has disposed of

(7) *„Die Lieferung":*
the sending
the consignment
the expedition

(8) *„versandfertig":*
OK to be sent
ready for delivery
on the ship

(9) *Sich bedanken:*
I am extremely grateful
We thank you
Thanks a lot

(10) *Sich auf etwas freuen:*
can't wait for
are very eager for
look forward to

 REDEWENDUNGEN

Einen Auftrag bestätigen

Thank you for your order.	*Vielen Dank für Ihre Bestellung.*
We are in receipt of your order no. 122.	*Wir bestätigen den Erhalt Ihrer Bestellung Nr. 122.*
We are pleased to acknowledge your order.	*Wir freuen uns Ihre Bestellung (hiermit) bestätigen zu können.*
We enclose the duplicate duly signed in acknowledgement of your order.	*Wir fügen das ordnungsgemäß unterzeichnete Doppel zur Bestätigung Ihrer Bestellung bei.*

Die Ausführung einer Bestellung bestätigen

We have pleasure in confirming that... .	*Wir freuen uns Ihnen bestätigen zu können, dass ... .*

Your order is already being pro-cessed / being dealt with.	Ihre Bestellung wird schon bearbeitet.
We have noted / recorded your order for… (goods).	Wir haben Ihre Bestellung über … (Waren) aufgenommen / notiert.
Our dispatch department is pro-cessing your order.	Unsere Versandabteilung bearbeitet Ihre Bestellung.

Einen Liefertermin bestätigen

Delivery will be made by… (date) as requested.	Die Lieferung wird wunschgemäß bis … (Datum) erfolgen.
Delivery will be made in accor-dance with / according to your instructions.	Die Auslieferung wird Ihren Anwei-sungen gemäß erfolgen.
We confirm that we are able to de-liver before the end of the month.	Wir bestätigen, dass wir vor Monats-ende liefern können.
The goods ordered are available for immediate delivery.	Die bestellten Waren können sofort geliefert werden.
We will inform you when the con-signment is ready for delivery.	Wir werden Sie informieren, sobald die Lieferung versandfertig ist.

Eine Verzögerung ankündigen

We should like to inform you / Please note that your order only reached us on… .	Wir möchten Ihnen mitteilen / Bitte beachten Sie, dass uns Ihre Bestellung erst am … erreicht hat.
We will require… days / weeks to process this order.	Wir werden … Tage / Wochen benötigen, um diese Bestellung zu bearbeiten.
Owing to an unfortunate delay, I regret to inform you that delivery can only be made from… onwards / in a week's time.	Wegen einer bedauerlichen Verzögerung muss ich Ihnen leider mitteilen, dass die Lieferung erst ab dem … / in einer Woche erfolgen kann.
Delivery has been delayed.	Die Auslieferung hat sich verzögert.

Schwierigkeiten einräumen

We regret to inform you that the goods / items ordered are out of stock / no longer in stock / no longer available.	Es tut uns leid Ihnen mitteilen zu müssen, dass die bestellten Waren / Teile nicht vorrätig / nicht mehr vorrätig / nicht mehr erhältlich sind.
Unfortunately…	Bedauerlicherweise / Leider …
I am afraid your order has been lost / has gone missing.	Ich fürchte, Ihre Bestellung kann nicht aufgefunden werden / ist verlorengegangen.
Could you possibly send us a dupli-cate / a copy of your order?	Könnten Sie uns möglicherweise ein Doppel / eine Kopie Ihrer Bestellung schicken?

Einen Ersatz anbieten

We can, however, offer you a substitute.

Our model no. 5 is very similar / of similar quality.

Wir können Ihnen jedoch einen Ersatz anbieten.

Unser Modell Nr. 5 ist sehr ähnlich / hat die gleiche Qualität.

 ## ANMERKUNGEN

→ Beachten Sie, dass die verschiedenen Abteilungen einer Firma **department** genannt werden, so z. B.: **the sales department** (Vertrieb / Verkaufsabteilung).

→ Merken Sie sich **to be of service to you**: Ihnen behilflich sein.

→ Beachten Sie das Fehlen des Artikels in der Redewendung **delivery will be made by 3rd June**: DIE Lieferung erfolgt bis (spätestens) 3. Juni.

 ## SIE SIND DRAN!

• We _____ to acknowledge your order no. 70 _____ 5th January. We _____ that delivery will _____ by 15th January.

• *Antworten Sie auf folgendes Fax:*
Re our order no. 56 please acknowledge receipt and confirm delivery by 19th May.

• _____ for your order no. 45. As requested we _____ the copy, _____ signed _____ acknowledgement. Your order is already _____ and will be ready for delivery _____ next week.

• *Bestätigen Sie den Auftrag mit der Nummer 95-SP8, aber teilen Sie dem Kunden mit, dass die Ware nicht vorrätig ist und dass sich die Auslieferung deshalb um drei Wochen verzögert.*

Lösung auf Seite 142

8 KOSTENVORANSCHLÄGE

Herr Müller beantwortet eine Anfrage bezüglich eines Kostenvoranschlags für verschiedene Telefonmodelle.

LUXI PHON
Magdeburger Straße 250 · 10785 Berlin

Boulton Manufacturing Ltd
45 Beech Road
Broughton
Somerset   15th April 19...

Your ref: 250MS / DK
Our ref: JM / RW

Dear Mr Stewart

(1) _____ your letter of 9th April, (2) _____
a detailed quotation for the models of telephones specified. Besides those
models that were on display at the International Telecommunications Fair,
(3) _____ other designs, as illustrated in our catalogue, also enclosed.
All our equipment is (4) _____ and comes with a five-year
guarantee. A number of accessories (5) _____ with some
of the models. Installation (6) _____ by any one of our
two thousand service centres located throughout Europe.
Furthermore, we are able to offer a 5% discount (7) _____
£2,000.
All models can be supplied, (8) _____ , 3 months from the
date on which we receive your firm order. Our cif prices are for sea / land
transport only; if you require the goods to be sent by air freight, this will be
charged at extra cost.

We look forward to receiving your order.

Yours sincerely

J. Müller

J Müller
Export Manager

Brief 12: Lösung auf Seite 134

Formulieren Sie seinen Brief mit Hilfe folgender Redewendungen:

(1) *„In Beantwortung":*
In reply to
Replying to
As a result of

(2) *„Wir freuen uns …*
beizulegen":
it is an honour to send you
we have pleasure in enclosing
we are pleased to include

(3) *Eine große Auswahl anbieten:*
we have a wide range of
we make plenty of
we are holding a sale of

(4) *Die Qualität hervorheben:*
the best
of a high standard
showing quality

(5) *„ist / sind erhältlich":*
is ready
are available
are disposable

(6) *Kostenlosen Anschluss anbieten:*
is carried out free of charge
is carried out gratuitously
is free

(7) *Bei größeren Aufträgen einen*
Rabatt gewähren:
for some orders exceeding
for all orders over
for any orders exceeding

(8) *„solange der Vorrat reicht":*
subject to availability
if possible
if in stock

 ## REDEWENDUNGEN

Sich auf einen Brief beziehen

In reply to your letter… .
Thank you for your enquiry about /
  your interest in… .
With reference to your letter of
  10th January… .

In Beantwortung Ihres Briefes … .
Wir bedanken uns für Ihre Anfrage
  bezüglich … / Ihr Interesse an … .
Wir beziehen uns auf Ihren Brief
  vom 10. Januar und … .

Unterlagen schicken

We have pleasure in enclosing… .
We are pleased to submit… for your
  approval.
our latest price list
our most recent catalogue
a detailed quotation for the goods
  specified

Wir freuen uns … beizufügen.
Wir freuen uns Ihnen … zur Ansicht
  vorlegen zu können.
unsere aktuelle Preisliste
unseren neuesten Katalog
einen genauen Kostenvoranschlag
  über die gewünschten Waren

Einen Rabatt oder Nachlaß gewähren

We are able to offer a 10% discount on all orders exceeding £20 in value / on repeat orders.

Wir können 10% Rabatt auf alle Bestellungen gewähren, die einen Wert von £20 übersteigen / ... auf alle Nachbestellungen anbieten.

We can make you a firm offer for... .

Wir können Ihnen ein festes Angebot über / für ... machen.

We can allow / offer a discount of 10%.

Wir können Ihnen einen 10%igen Rabatt einräumen / anbieten.

Your initial order is subject to a discount of 10%.

Auf Ihre Erstbestellung gewähren wir einen Rabatt von 10%.

This range is on offer at a special introductory price.

Diese Serie ist zu einem besonderen Einführungspreis im Angebot.

Den Lagerbestand beschreiben

All models can be supplied from stock.

Alle Modelle sind vorrätig.

Please let us have your order as soon as possible since supplies are limited.

Bitte schicken Sie uns Ihre Bestellung so bald wie möglich, da unsere Lagerbestände begrenzt sind.

Our stocks are depleted / sold out, but we can offer you a substitute.

Unsere Lagerbestände sind erschöpft / ausverkauft, aber wir können Ihnen Ersatz anbieten.

These goods are out of stock.

Diese Waren sind nicht vorrätig.

Vorbehalte äußern

subject to...

unter Vorbehalt, vorbehaltlich ...

subject to availability

solange der Vorrat reicht

subject to prior sale

Zwischenverkauf vorbehalten

subject to acceptance by the manager

nur mit Zustimmung des Geschäftsführers

subject to our receiving your order

nur mit / bei Auftragseingang

while stocks last

solange der Vorrat reicht

Prices are subject to change without notice.

Wir behalten uns Preisänderungen vor.

Zusätzliche Leistungen erwähnen

We have service centres all over the country.

Wir haben landesweit Dienstleistungszentren.

The equipment comes with optional accessories.

Für die Ausrüstung / Einrichtung gibt es verschiedenes Zubehör.

The goods carry / come with a one-year guarantee.

Auf die Waren / Produkte geben wir ein Jahr Garantie.

Installation is carried out free of charge.

Der Einbau / Anschluss ist kostenlos / gebührenfrei.

Zahlungsarten und Preise

cif prices / cost insurance freight	*Preise für Kosten, Versicherung und Fracht*
to be charged at extra cost	*zuzüglich berechnet werden*
terms of payment 30 days net	*Zahlungsbedingungen: netto innerhalb*
	30 Tagen

 ## ANMERKUNGEN

→ Der englische Ausdruck **a number of (accessories)** kann mit „eine gewisse Anzahl" oder „einige" übersetzt werden.

→ Beachten Sie, dass die Passivformulierung **if you require the goods to be sent** häufig in formellen Geschäftsbriefen verwendet wird.

→ Unterscheiden Sie: **of a high standard** (mit Artikel) und **of good quality** (ohne Artikel).

 ## SIE SIND DRAN!

• In _____ your inquiry of 5th December, we are pleased to _____ a detailed quotation _____ the goods specified. We can allow a 3% discount _____ all orders _____ £50. Prices are _____ change without _____ .

• We are pleased _____ a quotation _____ the renovation of your premises. The work carried out _____ a guarantee of one year _____ your prior approval of the completed renovation. We enclose our most _____ catalogue to give you an indication of the materials available. We also _____ our _____ price list.

• In _____ your inquiry of 1st September we are pleased _____ the requested quotation _____ goods specified. This range is a special _____ offer, with a 5% discount _____ your initial order. If you wish to take advantage _____ this offer, please fill _____ the _____ form.

• With _____ to your enquiry _____ 8th January, we have pleasure _____ enclosing a quotation _____ the goods specified. Please let _____ have your order as soon as possible, since _____ are limited.

⊶ Lösung auf Seite 142

9 ZAHLUNGSBEDINGUNGEN

Herr Müller schreibt einer Kundin, Frau Mary Donovan, die Luxiphon einen Großauftrag erteilen möchte.

LUXI PHON
Magdeburger Straße 250 • 10785 Berlin

Mrs Mary Donovan
Northern Supplies Ltd
56 High Street
Sheffield
YORKSHIRE NW36 SJ2   8th May 19...

_____

(2) _____ your (3) _____ regarding our
(4) _____ . (5) _____ 30 days net, but we can allow
you (6) _____ for (7) _____
Payment (8) _____ by irrevocable letter of credit or
order cheque.

(9) _____ your initial order.

(10) _____

J. Müller

J Müller
Export Manager

Brief 13: Lösung auf Seite 134

Helfen Sie ihm, die Zahlungsbedingungen zu erläutern:

(1) *Die Anrede:*
   Dear Mrs Donovan
   Dear Mary
   Dear Madam

(2) *„Wir beziehen uns auf":*
   We refer to
   With reference to
   As regards

(3) *„kürzliche Anfrage":*
   recent inquiry
   latest demand
   last question

(4) *„Zahlungsbedingungen":*
   terms for paying
   rules of payment
   conditions of payment

(5) *Die Zahlungsbedingungen*
   angeben:
   We require
   Our terms are
   You must pay

(6) *„ein Zahlungsziel von zwei*
   Monaten":
   two months' credit
   two months' debt
   a delay of two months

(7) *„Nachbestellungen":*
   other orders
   subsequent orders
   firm orders

(8) *Die Zahlung „sollte … erfolgen":*
   must be done
   is to take place
   should be made

(9) *„Wir freuen uns auf den Erhalt":*
   We look forward to receiving
   We are waiting to receive
   We expect to receive

(10) *Die Grußformel:*
   Regards
   Yours faithfully
   Yours sincerely

 REDEWENDUNGEN

Die Zahlungsbedingungen angeben

Our conditions / terms of payment are as follows:	*Unsere Zahlungsbedingungen lauten / sind folgende:*
Payment should be made by… .	*Die Zahlung sollte per … erfolgen.*
(irrevocable) letter of credit	*(unwiderrufliches) Akkreditiv*
bank transfer	*Banküberweisung*
banker's draft / bank draft	*Bankwechsel*
cheque	*Scheck*
cash on delivery	*Zahlung gegen Nachnahme*
cash with order	*Zahlung bei Auftragserteilung*
cash in advance	*Vorauszahlung*
direct debit	*Direktabbuchung*
quarterly / monthly payment	*vierteljährliche / monatliche Zahlung*

payment at sight	*Zahlung bei Vorlage*
cash against documents	*Kasse gegen Dokumente*
pro forma invoice	*Zahlung durch Proforma-Rechnung*
International Money Order (IMO)	*internationale Postanweisung*
(current) exchange rate	*aktueller Wechselkurs*
VAT (value added tax)	*Mehrwertsteuer*
tax free, duty free	*steuerfrei, zollfrei*
exclusive of tax	*ohne Steuer / Steuer nicht inbegriffen*
inclusive of tax	*inklusive Steuer / Steuer inbegriffen*

Sich nach Sonderkonditionen erkundigen

Are you able to allow a discount?	*Können Sie einen Nachlass gewähren?*
Could you grant us a preferential rate for this bulk order?	*Können Sie uns für eine Bestellung in dieser Größenordnung einen Sonderpreis gewähren?*

Einen Zahlungsaufschub / Kredit gewähren oder ablehnen

We can allow you 2 months' credit.	*Wir können Ihnen ein Zahlungsziel von zwei Monaten gewähren.*
We do not give credit.	*Wir gewähren keinen Kredit.*
We are not in a position to offer credit.	*Wir sind nicht in der Lage Kredit zu gewähren.*
Our terms of payment are 30 days net.	*Unsere Zahlungsbedingungen lauten: Zahlung innerhalb 30 Tagen ohne Abzug / netto.*

Um Begleichung einer Rechnung bitten

Enclosed is our invoice amounting to… .	*Unsere Rechnung über … liegt bei.*
We should be grateful if you would forward your remittance in settlement of the enclosed invoice.	*Wir wären Ihnen dankbar, wenn Sie den Betrag zur Begleichung der beiliegenden Rechnung überweisen könnten.*

Eine Zahlung leisten

We have pleasure in enclosing… .	*Wir freuen uns, Ihnen … zuschicken zu können.*
an International Money Order (IMO) for…	*eine internationale Postanweisung über …*
your bill of exchange / a cheque for…	*Ihren Wechsel / einen Scheck über …*
Enclosed is our banker's draft for…	*Unser Bankwechsel über … liegt bei.*
Our bank has been instructed to transfer the agreed 10% deposit.	*Unsere Bank ist angewiesen die vereinbarte Anzahlung von 10% zu überweisen.*

As payment of pro forma invoice no. …, we enclose a draft on… .	*Zur Begleichung der Proforma-Rechnung Nr. … legen wir einen Wechsel über … bei.*

Den Zahlungseingang bestätigen

We are pleased to confirm receipt of… .	*Wir freuen uns den Eingang von … zu bestätigen.*
Thank you for your cheque for… .	*Wir bedanken uns für Ihren Scheck über … .*

Eine Gutschriftsanzeige schicken

Please forward a credit note for the sum of… .	*Bitte senden Sie uns eine Gutschrifts-anzeige über die Summe von … .*
We enclose a credit note for the sum of… .	*Wir legen eine Gutschriftsanzeige über die Summe von … bei.*

Ein Kundenkonto besitzen

I should like to open an account with you.	*Ich möchte ein Konto bei Ihnen eröffnen.*
Could you possibly forward your account details, including your account number and credit card number?	*Könnten Sie uns bitte Informationen über Ihr Konto zugehen lassen, einschließlich Ihrer Konto- und Kreditkartennummer?*

Ein Formular ausfüllen

Please write in block capitals.	*Bitte in Blockschrift schreiben.*
made payable to	*zahlbar an*
amount due	*fälliger Betrag*
amount in words	*Betrag in Worten*

 ANMERKUNGEN

→ Die Redewendung **payment should be made** klingt viel höflicher als „payment must be made" und wird deshalb vorzugsweise benutzt.

→ Der Artikel vor **payment** (s. o.) entfällt, weil hier keine spezielle Zahlung ge-meint ist, sondern Zahlungen im Allgemeinen.

→ Bitte beachten Sie die unterschiedliche Schreibweise: **cheque** (BE) und **check** (AE).

 **SIE SIND DRAN!**

- Our usual _____ are 60 days _____ . We can _____ you 1 month's further _____ for repeat _____ . Payment _____ by bank transfer.

- _____ is our invoice _____ £500. Would you kindly _____ your remittance _____ of the above as soon as possible.

- We _____ enclosing our _____ draft _____ £200 _____ settlement of the enclosed invoice no. 334. Please _____ receipt _____ return _____ post.

- We are not in a _____ to offer credit, but we can _____ a discount _____ all orders _____ £300.

- We _____ with thanks _____ banker's draft for £572, sent in payment of order no. 910.
We _____ to receiving your next order.

Lösung auf Seite 142

10 LIEFERBEDINGUNGEN

Herr Müller erklärt einer amerikanischen Kundin die Lieferbedingungen für eine Warensendung.

Dear Ms Webster

(1) _____ your order No. 33. (2) _____ within
two months of (3) _____ . (4) _____, the
consignment will be transported (5) _____ fob from Birmingham
to your warehouse in Atlanta, Georgia.

Our prices are cif for sea / land transport to Georgia.
(6) _____ more rapid delivery, (7) _____ for
the goods to be sent by air freight, but (8) _____ .
Insurance is (9) _____ .

(10) _____ and will be pleased to answer any further
queries you might have regarding the shipment.

Yours truly

J. Müller

J Müller
Export Manager

⌐━━⌐ Brief 14: Lösung auf Seite 135

Helfen Sie ihm nun die Lieferbedingungen mit Hilfe folgender Begriffe zu formulieren:

(1) *„Wir beziehen uns auf"*:
  As regards
  We refer to
  We have referred to

(2) *Welche ist die richtige Zeit-
form?*
  Delivery will be made
  Delivery has been made
  Delivery would be made

(3) *Zwei Monate nach „Erhalt Ihrer*
    Bestellung":
    your order
    the ship's arrival
    receipt of your order

(4) *„Wie vereinbart":*
    As arranged
    As convenient
    As you know

(5) *Transportbedingungen:*
    by train and ship
    by rail and sea freight
    in a train and on a ship

(6) *„Falls Sie … benötigen":*
    If you require
    Should you be in need of
    If you must have

(7) *Eine Dienstleistung vorschlagen:*
    we can allow
    we have arranged
    we can arrange

(8) *Zusatzkosten erwähnen:*
    this will be charged at extra cost
    this will be charged to your bankers
    this is very costly

(9) *Zahlungsbedingungen nennen:*
    payable on arrival
    payable by you
    optional

(10) *Sich für den Auftrag bedanken:*
    Thanks a lot for your order
    We look forward to your next
     order
    We thank you for your custom

 REDEWENDUNGEN

Lieferfristen mitteilen

Delivery will take four months.	*Bis zur Auslieferung wird es vier Monate dauern.*
The consignment is ready for immediate delivery.	*Die Sendung ist versandbereit.*
Delivery can be made from stock.	*Lieferung ab Lager.*
The items are in stock and should be ready for despatch by next Monday.	*Die Artikel sind vorrätig und dürften bis kommenden Montag zur Auslieferung versandfertig sein.*
Delivery will be made within two months.	*Die Lieferung wird innerhalb zwei Monaten erfolgen.*

Das Transportmittel mitteilen

As arranged, the consignment will be transported by air / rail / sea freight.	*Wie abgesprochen wird die Lieferung per Luft- / Bahn- / Seefracht transportiert werden.*
We will despatch the goods to-morrow by air freight.	*Wir werden die Waren morgen per Luftfracht verschicken.*

Die Versandbedingungen angeben

Our prices are… .
EXW – ex works, ex warehouse
FCA – free carrier
FOB – free on board
free / franco domicile
CPT – carriage paid to…
CIF – cost, insurance, freight
CFR – cost and freight
CIP – carriage and insurance
   paid to…
DDP – delivery duty paid
DAF – delivered at frontier

Unsere Preise gelten … .
ab Werk, ab Lager
frei Frachtführer
frei an Bord
frei Haus
frachtfrei bis …
Kosten, Versicherung, Fracht
Kosten und Fracht
frachtfrei versichert bis …

geliefert verzollt
geliefert Grenze

Die Lieferadresse mitteilen

Please note that delivery should be
   made to the following address.
Would you please deliver to the
   following address?
Please note the new address of our
   offices.

*Bitte beachten Sie, dass die Lieferung
   an folgende Adresse erfolgen soll.*
*Würden Sie bitte an folgende
   Adresse liefern?*
*Bitte beachten Sie die neue Adresse
   unserer Büros.*

Den Versand anzeigen

We are pleased to inform you that
   we have despatched… today,
   in accordance with your order.
As agreed, the goods will be delivered to you on Monday
   morning.
Order no. … will be ready for delivery as from 5th May. Please
   advise as to how you will take
   delivery of the goods.

*Es freut uns Ihnen mitteilen zu können,
   dass wir heute gemäß Ihrer
   Bestellung … ausgeliefert haben.*
*Wie abgesprochen werden Ihnen
   die Waren Montagmorgen zuge-
   stellt.*
*Die Bestellung Nr. … wird ab 5. Mai
   versandbereit sein. Bitte teilen
   Sie uns mit, in welcher Form Sie
   die Lieferung entgegennehmen.*

Einen Lieferverzug mitteilen

Owing to… we are unable to deliver
   your order no. … before 7th June.

Unless we receive instructions from
   you to the contrary, we will assume
   that your order still stands.

*Wegen / Aufgrund … sind wir nicht
   in der Lage Ihre Bestellung Nr. …
   vor 7. Juni auszuliefern.*
*Falls wir nichts Gegenteiliges von
   Ihnen hören, nehmen wir an, dass
   die Bestellung noch gültig ist.*

Die Versandart beschreiben

The goods will be delivered in hermetically sealed, shock-proof crates.	*Die Waren werden in hermetisch versiegelten, stoßfesten Kisten verschickt (werden).*
The documentation requested has been sent to you… .	*Die angeforderten Unterlagen wurden Ihnen … zugeschickt.*
under separate cover	*mit getrennter Post*
by registered post	*per Einschreiben*
by messenger / by courier	*per Boten / per Eilboten*

 ANMERKUNGEN

→ Beachten Sie, dass in Redewendungen wie **Delivery will be made / The consignment will be transported / This will be charged** das Passiv benutzt wird. Wegen seines nicht so persönlichen, dafür aber formelleren Aspekts wird in Geschäftsbriefen diese Form dem Aktiv vorgezogen.

→ Merken Sie sich die Redewendung **is payable by you** d. h. „geht / gehen zu Ihren Lasten". Diese Formulierung, ebenfalls im Passiv, ist auf die Handelskorrespondenz beschränkt und ist höflicher als „Sie müssen … zahlen".

 **SIE SIND DRAN!**

• *Schreiben Sie Herrn Müller und präzisieren Sie die Lieferbedingungen für die von Ihnen bestellten Waren: Lieferung vor 15. 11. per See- und Schienenfracht, ab Fabrik Luxiphon bis zu Ihrem Lager, geliefert verzollt.*

• We _____ your order _____ 500 pairs of green socks. The items are _____ stock and should be ready _____ despatch by next week. Delivery _____ made _____ one month of processing the order.

• Owing _____ problems _____ our manufacturing plant, we are _____ to deliver your order no. 77. _____ we receive _____ from you _____ the contrary, we will _____ that your order still stands.

Lösung auf Seite 143

66   TERMS OF DELIVERY

11 ZAHLUNGSERINNERUNGEN

Herr Müller stellt eines Tages fest, dass einige Kunden bereits vor drei Monaten ausgeführte Aufträge noch nicht bezahlt haben. Es wäre ihm lieber, wenn er diese Zahlungserinnerungen nicht schicken müsste!

LUXI PHON
Magdeburger Straße 250 • 10785 Berlin

Mr Jason Hughes   20th October 19…
Scientific Ltd
155 Birmingham Avenue
Cleveland Ohio 44321
USA

(1) _____

We would like to (2) _____ our invoice No.254 dated September 5th.
(3) _____ payment, (4) _____ if you would
(5) _____ as soon as possible. (6) _____ the
amount due, please (7) _____ .

(8) _____

J. Müller

J Müller
Export Manager

⊶—⚹ Brief 15: Lösung auf Seite 135

Helfen Sie ihm beim Aufsetzen seines Mahnschreibens an seinen amerikanischen Kunden und verwenden Sie folgende Begriffe:

(1) *Die Anrede:*
Dear Jason
Dear Mr Hughes
Dear Sir or Madam

(2) *Auf etwas hinweisen:*
indicate
mention
draw your attention to

(3) *Mitteilen, dass die Zahlung noch nicht erfolgt ist:*
As we are still waiting for
As we are in desperate need of
As we have not yet received

(4) *Um etwas bitten:*
we should be grateful
we would be most obliged
we would be happy

(5) *Um Zahlung bitten:*
send the money
forward your remittance
deal with the problem

(6) *„Falls Sie ... schon überwiesen haben":*
If you are thinking of sending
If you will have sent
If you have already sent

(7) *„betrachten Sie dieses Schreiben als gegenstandslos":*
forget about this letter
ignore this reminder
do not take account of this note

(8) *Die Grußformel:*
Yours sincerely
Yours truly
Yours faithfully

 REDEWENDUNGEN

Sich auf die Rechnung beziehen

Our invoice, of which we enclose a copy, was sent to you on... (date).
We are writing in connection with your outstanding account of... .
We would like to draw your attention to our invoice of... (date).

Beiliegend eine Kopie unserer Rechnung, die Ihnen am ... (Datum) zuging.
Wir beziehen uns auf den noch ausstehenden Betrag von ... .
Wir möchten Sie hiermit auf unsere Rechnung vom ... (Datum) hinweisen.

Eine Zahlungserinnerung schicken

As we have not yet received payment, we would be grateful if you would forward your remittance as soon as possible.

Da wir noch keine Zahlung erhalten haben, wären wir Ihnen für eine umgehende Begleichung der Rechnung dankbar.

As the account has not yet been cleared, could you please send your remittance as soon as possible?

Da Ihr Konto noch nicht ausgeglichen ist, bitten wir Sie, Ihre Überweisung baldmöglichst vorzunehmen.

As no advice of payment has been received from our bank, we would be glad if you would arrange for settlement of this invoice.

Da wir von unserer Bank noch keine Zahlungsmitteilung erhalten haben, wären wir Ihnen dankbar, wenn Sie die Rechnung begleichen könnten.

May we remind you our terms are 30 days net. Kindly send your remittance as soon as possible.

Wir möchten Sie daran erinnern, dass unsere Bedingungen 30 Tage netto lauten. Bitte begleichen Sie die Rechnung baldmöglichst.

Falls der Kunde die Rechnung schon beglichen hat

Should you have already settled the account, please disregard this reminder.

Sollten Sie die Rechnung schon beglichen haben, so betrachten Sie diese Zahlungserinnerung bitte als gegenstandslos.

If you have already sent the required amount, please ignore this reminder.

Sollten Sie den betreffenden Betrag schon gezahlt haben, so ignorieren Sie bitte diese Zahlungserinnerung.

Eine zweite Mahnung schicken

We wish to remind you that our invoice no. X dated… is still unpaid / outstanding and ask you to give the matter your immediate attention.

Wir möchten daran erinnern, dass unsere Rechnung Nr. X vom … noch nicht beglichen wurde, und bitten Sie, die Angelegenheit umgehend zu erledigen.

Having received no reply to our letter of… in which we reminded you that we are still awaiting settlement of our invoice no. X, we must request payment of the amount due without further delay.

Da wir keine Antwort auf unser Schreiben vom … erhielten, in dem wir darauf hinwiesen, dass die Rechnung Nr. X noch nicht beglichen wurde, bitten wir Sie den ausstehenden Betrag umgehend zu begleichen.

We enclose a statement of your account. We feel sure that its settlement has been overlooked, but having already sent one reminder, we must insist that payment be made within the next seven days.

Wir fügen einen Kontoauszug bei. Sicher handelt es sich (hierbei) um ein Versehen Ihrerseits; da wir aber schon eine Zahlungserinnerung geschickt haben, müssen wir darauf bestehen, dass die Zahlung innerhalb der nächsten sieben Tage erfolgt.

Eine letzte Mahnung schicken

Despite two reminders sent to you on… and…, the amount of our invoice no. X is still outstanding, and is now three months overdue. As we have received no reply from you, we shall have to take legal proceedings unless payment reaches us within the next seven days.

Obwohl Ihnen am … und am … zwei Zahlungserinnerungen zugingen, steht der Betrag unserer Rechnung Nr. X noch immer aus und ist nun bereits seit drei Monaten überfällig. Da wir keine Antwort von Ihnen erhielten, werden wir rechtliche Schritte (gegen Sie) einleiten müssen, falls die Rechnung nicht innerhalb der nächsten sieben Tage beglichen wird.

Unless we have received your remittance within seven days, we shall have to hand the matter over to our solicitors.

Sollten wir Ihre Zahlung nicht innerhalb sieben Tagen erhalten, werden wir die Angelegenheit unseren Rechtsanwälten übergeben müssen.

Antwort auf ein Mahnschreiben

I regret to inform you that we can find no trace of invoice no. 27. We would be obliged if you could send us a duplicate of the invoice so that we can proceed with the necessary payment.

Ich muss Ihnen leider mitteilen, dass sich die Rechnung Nr. 27 nicht auffinden läßt. Wir wären Ihnen dankbar, wenn Sie uns eine Kopie dieser Rechnung zugehen lassen könnten, so dass wir die nötige Zahlung veranlassen können.

The delay in the settlement of our outstanding account no. 38G12 has been caused by a computer error in our accounts department.

Die Verzögerung bei der Begleichung des offen stehenden Kontos Nr. 38G12 wurde durch einen Computerfehler in unserer Rechnungsabteilung hervorgerufen.

Please accept our apologies for the inconvenience caused, and rest assured that you will be receiving our remittance shortly.

Wir entschuldigen uns für die Ihnen entstandenen Ungelegenheiten und versichern Ihnen, dass die Zahlung in Kürze bei Ihnen eingehen wird.

We apologize for the delay in our settlement of your invoice no. 63, but we have recently experienced some cash flow problems. We should be grateful if you could allow us a further credit of 30 days.

Wir entschuldigen uns für die Verzögerung bei der Zahlung Ihrer Rechnung Nr. 63, aber es ergaben sich in letzter Zeit einige Cash-flow-Probleme. Wir wären Ihnen dankbar, wenn Sie uns einen weiteren Kredit von 30 Tagen einräumen könnten.

 **ANMERKUNGEN**

→ Beachten Sie, dass **may we...** wie das deutsche „dürfen wir … „ benutzt wird, um eventuell unangenehme Aufforderungen zu entschärfen oder sie höflicher zu formulieren. **We draw your attention to...** wäre die direktere, aber nicht so höfliche Möglichkeit auf etwas hinzuweisen.

→ Statt der Formulierung **we would be grateful...** findet man auch **we should be grateful...** mit exakt der gleichen Bedeutung. Diese Form des Konjunktiv ist nur in der 1. Person **I / we** möglich, wird aber im modernen Englisch zunehmend ungebräuchlicher. In der 2. und 3. Person wird in jedem Fall nur **would** verwendet, also:
I / We would / should like to inform you...
He / She would like to inform you...

 **SIE SIND DRAN!**

• As we _____ received payment _____ our invoice no. 609, we would be grateful if you would forward _____ as _____ possible.

• _____ previous reminders your account is _____ outstanding. _____ payment reaches us _____ the next seven days, we shall have to take _____ .

• *Bestätigen Sie den Erhalt einer Zahlungserinnerung für die Rechnung Nr. 703B. Weisen Sie darauf hin, dass diese Rechnung schon beglichen wurde und dass es sich um einen Buchungsfehler handeln muss.*

⚬═╼ Lösung auf Seite 143

12 VERHANDLUNGEN UND VEREINBARUNGEN

Beim Durchgehen der Post stößt Herr Müller auf eine unerwartete Anfrage. Panorama, eine amerikanische Firma, die Anrufbeantworter herstellt, bietet ein Partnerschaftsabkommen an: Luxiphon soll die amerikanischen Anrufbeantworter auf den europäischen Markt bringen; als Gegenleistung will Panorama den Vertrieb von Luxiphon-Produkten in den USA übernehmen.

—— Panorama Ltd ——
1150 Grand Boulevard • Los Angeles California 90041 • USA

Luxiphon
Magdeburger Str. 250
10785 Berlin
Germany   25th April 19…

Our ref: TS / PL 314

Dear Sir or Madam

We are manufacturers of telephone answering machines and
(1) _____ a European manufacturer of compatible products
with a view to entering into a commercial partnership.
We would like to offer our services as commercial agents for your products in
the United States, (2) _____ your representation of our products on
the European market. Please find enclosed a brochure describing our company.

As we are sure (3) _____ , the US market offers excellent potential
for your type of product, and (4) _____ that you will appreciate
how much (5) _____ from such a partnership. As for ourselves,
we have reason to believe that the market (6) _____ in Europe
for our products and consider that the best way (7) _____ is to
achieve a commercial presence via a European company.

We hope you will (8) _____ , and look forward to your reply.

Yours truly

D. Southampton

Mr T Southampton
Export Manager

Brief 16: Lösung auf Seite 135

Vervollständigen Sie das Geschäftsangebot, das Panorama Herrn Müller zugeschickt hat:

(1) *„Wir sind auf der Suche nach":*
would like to meet
are seeking
will be contacting

(2) *„als Gegenleistung für":*
as an exchange for
in exchange with
in exchange for

(3) *„ist Ihnen bekannt":*
you are aware
you must know
you bear in mind

(4) *Eine positive Antwort voraussetzen:*
we assume
we realise
we feel confident

(5) *„Ihre Firma könnte … profitieren":*
your company could benefit
you could gain
your turnover would increase

(6) *Der Markt „öffnet sich":*
is opening up
has started
will be good

(7) *Von einer Situation profitieren:*
to win
to compete
to take advantage of this
   opportunity

(8) *Das Angebot in Erwägung ziehen:*
look into this
give this proposal your kind
   consideration
give this your immediate attention

REDEWENDUNGEN

Sich auf die Kontaktaufnahme beziehen

Having recently visited your stand … .
I was given your name by Mr… .
The Chamber of Commerce suggested I contact you.
We met / were introduced at the
   Frankfurt Book Fair.

Da ich kürzlich Ihren Stand besuchte, … .
Herr … nannte mir Ihren Namen.
Die Handelskammer riet mir mit
   Ihnen Kontakt aufzunehmen.
Wir lernten uns auf der Frankfurter
   Buchmesse kennen (Wir wurden
   einander auf … vorgestellt).

Die eigene Gesellschaft vorstellen

We are retailers of… .
We are manufacturers of… .
We are a distribution company
   specialising in electrical goods.
We are specialists in marine
   insurance.

Wir sind Einzelhändler für … .
Wir stellen … her.
Wir sind eine Vertriebsgesellschaft, die
   sich auf elektrische Geräte spezialisiert.
Wir sind Spezialisten für Seeversicherungen.

We are a trading company specialising in the promotion, marketing and sales of hi-fi equipment to Middle Eastern countries.

Wir sind eine Handelsgesellschaft, die sich auf Werbung, Vermarktung und Verkauf von Hi-Fi-Equipment / -Anlagen für den Mittleren Osten spezialisiert.

We are one of the leading German suppliers of pharmaceutical products to the Third World.

Wir sind einer der führenden deutschen Lieferanten für pharmazeutische Produkte in die Dritte Welt.

Die Art des Abkommens näher erläutern

We would like to form a partnership.

Wir möchten eine Partnerschaft / Teilhaberschaft aufbauen.

We would be interested in an agency agreement to cover the whole of Eastern Europe.

Wir wären an einem Vertretervertrag für ganz Osteuropa interessiert.

We are interested in offering our services to you for the distribution of your products in this part of the world.

Wir möchten Ihnen unsere Dienste beim Vertrieb Ihrer Produkte, in diesem Teil der Erde, anbieten.

We would be interested in forming a joint venture with your company.

Wir sind an einem Jointventure mit Ihrer Firma interessiert.

Ein Angebot machen

We would like to offer our services as... .

Wir möchten unsere Dienste als ... anbieten.

We would like to suggest a collaboration in the development and commercialisation of new technologies.

Wir möchten eine Zusammenarbeit, bei der Entwicklung und Vermarktung neuer Technologien, vorschlagen.

Auf günstige Handelsbedingungen hinweisen

If your company is interested in starting or increasing sales to... (country), this presents a good opportunity.

Falls Ihre Firma daran interessiert ist, den Vertrieb in... (Land) aufzunehmen oder zu intensivieren, bietet sich hiermit eine gute Gelegenheit dazu.

There is potentially a very good market for quality leather shoes in this part of the world.

In diesem Teil der Erde gibt es für Qualitätslederschuhe einen potenziell hervorragenden Markt.

There is much demand for your type of product here.

Nach Produkten wie Ihrem besteht hier eine große Nachfrage.

The market is expanding / opening up / booming / beginning to pick up.

Der Markt expandiert / öffnet sich / boomt / erholt sich allmählich wieder.

The continuing consumer boom in... (country) has created a promising market for...(product).

Die anhaltende Hochkonjunktur in ... (Land), hat einen vielversprechenden Markt für ... (Produkt) geschaffen.

Um Antwort bitten

We hope you will give this proposal your kind consideration.

We look forward to receiving your comments on the above / on this proposal.

In case you are unable to help us with this proposal, we would be grateful if you could put us in touch with a company that may be interested.

Wir hoffen, dass dieser Vorschlag Ihr Interesse findet.

Wir freuen uns auf Ihre Beurteilung des oben genannten / dieses Vorschlags.

Sollten Sie nicht in der Lage sein, auf unseren Vorschlag einzugehen, wären wir Ihnen dankbar, wenn Sie uns mit einer Firma in Kontakt bringen könnten, die eventuell daran interessiert wäre.

 ## ANMERKUNGEN

→ Beachten Sie die ing-Form in: **with a view to enterING into...** (im Hinblick auf einen Einstieg in ...).

→ Merken Sie sich das Verb **to be aware (of)**: „sich einer Sache bewusst sein, über etwas unterrichtet sein"; die betontere Form **you are not unaware (of the fact that...)** muss im Deutschen, wegen ihrer doppelten Verneinung, mit „Sie sind sich sicherlich (der Tatsache) bewusst, dass ..." übersetzt werden.

→ Beachten Sie die Redewendung **to feel confident**: „überzeugt / sich sicher sein".

 ## SIE SIND DRAN!

• We are a trading company _____ in the _____ and _____ of construction equipment _____ the Asian market. We _____ an agency agreement for the commercialisation of your products _____ this part of the world.

• We are retailers _____ video games and _____ interested in acting as agents _____ you in Western Africa. We _____ our brochure detailing our activities. We look _____ your comments _____ this proposal.

• We _____ distribution company _____ computers and _____ be interested in a partnership _____ the distribution of your products, to cover the whole _____ Northern Europe. If you are interested _____ this proposal, please get in _____ with us as soon as possible.

Lösung auf Seite 143

13 VERTRÄGE AUFSETZEN

Herr Müller legt die Vertragsbedingungen der Handelsvertretung mit der amerikanischen Firma Panorama fest.

LUXI PHON
Magdeburger Straße 250 · 10785 Berlin

Mr T Southampton
Panorama Ltd
1150 Grand Boulevard
Los Angeles
CA 90041 USA   12th May 19...

Your ref: TS / PL 314
Our ref: JM / S 67

Dear Mr Southampton

Agency Agreement

(1) _____ our telephone conversation of Thursday,
I am pleased to confirm the agency agreement giving you
(2) _____ for our products in the United States.

(3) _____ two copies of our terms for the agency
agreement. Would you please (4) _____ and return them to
me, (5) _____ any comments or amendments you would like
to make regarding the contents? (6) _____ concerning the
conditions of the agency agreement (7) _____ .

I look forward to (8) _____ to discuss the final contract, and
hope this is the beginning of a long and mutually beneficial association.

Yours truly

J. Müller

J Müller
Export Manager

Encs

Brief 17: Lösung auf Seite 135 / 136

Schreiben Sie Herrn Müllers Brief mit Hilfe nachfolgender Begriffe:

(1) *„Bezug nehmend auf":*
   With reference to
   To refer to
   Having referred to

(2) *Eine Alleinvertretung vor-*
   schlagen:
   exclusive representation
   sole agency
   only to represent

(3) *„Anbei finden Sie":*
   Inside please find
   Enclosed are
   You will find joined

(4) *Um Unterzeichnung beider*
   Exemplare bitten:
   sign two copies
   sign the examples twice
   sign both copies

(5) *„zusammen mit":*
   together with
   besides
   further to

(6) *„Für weitere Fragen":*
   For all other information
   If you have more questions
   Should you have any further
    queries

(7) *„ … stehe ich Ihnen gerne zur*
   Verfügung":
   I am to be disposed of
   I am in your disposition
   please do not hesitate to contact me

(8) *„unser baldiges Treffen":*
   our next meeting
   our forthcoming meeting
   meeting us soon

 REDEWENDUNGEN

Den Vertrag bestätigen

With reference to our discussion /
  your letter / our telephone conversation, we are pleased to confirm… .
the agency agreement
our partnership
our joint venture

the franchise

Bezug nehmend auf unser Gespräch /
  Ihren Brief / unser Telefongespräch
  freuen wir uns, … zu bestätigen.
der Vertretervertrag
unsere Partnerschaft
unser Jointventure / Gemeinschafts-
  unternehmen
die Franchise / das Alleinverkaufsrecht

Um Unterzeichnung bitten

Enclosed are two copies of the
  contract.
Would you please sign both copies
  and return one to me?
Enc(s), Encl(s)

In der Anlage finden Sie zwei Kopien
  des Vertrags.
Unterzeichnen Sie bitte beide Kopien
  und senden Sie eine an mich zurück.
Anlage(n)

Schlussformeln

If you have any further queries regarding the conditions of the contract please do not hesitate to contact me.	*Sollten Sie weitere Fragen zu den Vertragsbedingungen haben, stehe ich Ihnen gerne zur Verfügung.*
I look forward to our forthcoming meeting.	*Ich freue mich auf unser baldiges Treffen.*
I hope this is the beginning of a long and mutually beneficial association (between our two companies).	*Ich hoffe, dies ist der Anfang einer langen und (für beide Firmen) fruchtbaren Zusammenarbeit.*
Please let us know within 3 weeks if these terms are acceptable.	*Bitte geben Sie uns innerhalb der nächsten drei Wochen Bescheid, ob Sie mit diesen Bedingungen einverstanden sind.*

Im nebenstehenden Vertrag sind alle in dieser Art von Dokumenten häufig vorkommenden Elemente fettgedruckt.

AGREEMENT No. 176

General conditions

1. Panorama Ltd (**hereafter referred to as** „The Agent") must work **exclusively** for Luxiphon (hereafter referred to as „The Company").

2. The Agent **must undertake** not to work for The Company's competitors.

3. The Agent must **confine his activities to the area of** the United States of America.

4. **The Agent's task is to** represent The Company in all ways necessary **to promote the commercial success** of The Company's products in the United States, including presenting catalogues and giving demonstrations to customers, carrying out marketing and advertising campaigns, and managing the importation, sales and distribution of all such products.

VERTRAG NR. 176

Allgemeine Bedingungen

1. *Die „Panorama Ltd" (nachfolgend „der Agent" genannt) darf ausschließlich für „Luxiphon" (nachfolgend „die Firma" genannt) tätig werden.*

2. *Der Agent muss sich verpflichten, nicht für die Konkurrenz der Firma zu arbeiten.*

3. *Der Agent muss seine Tätigkeit auf das Gebiet der USA beschränken.*

4. *Aufgabe des Agenten ist es, die Firma mit allen Mitteln zu repräsentieren, die für einen wirtschaftlichen Erfolg der Firmenprodukte in den USA notwendig sind. Dies schließt die Präsentation von Katalogen, Kundenvorführungen, die Durchführung von Marketing- und Werbekampagnen sowie Import, Verkauf und Vertrieb all jener Produkte ein.*

5. The Company **is prepared to spend an average of** DM 150,000 per year on advertising. The Company **will advise on** marketing and advertising of the goods.

6. **The contract is limited initially to** 2 years, and **may be renewed** based on **an annual evaluation** of the Agent's performance.

7. The contract **may be cancelled by either party subject to 3 months' notice**.

8. There will be a **trial period of** 6 months at the end of which either party may cancel the contract subject to one month's notice.

9. Goods are sold **on a commission basis,** but The Company is prepared **to take on** part of the administration and marketing costs. The Company's **normal rate of commission** for overseas representatives is 20 % of the turnover. This commission is payable on all orders placed through The Agent or his / her intermediaries, and is to include **any expenses** The Agent **incurs, provided** The Agent sends the Company full details of such expenses and the **corresponding receipts**. The commission will be **paid quarterly**.

.../...

5. Die Firma ist bereit, durchschnittlich DM 150.000 pro Jahr für Werbezwecke auszugeben. Die Firma wird beim Vertrieb der Produkte und bei deren Werbung beratend tätig sein.

6. Der Vertrag ist zunächst auf zwei Jahre befristet und kann auf der Grundlage einer alljährlichen Bewertung der Tätigkeit des Agenten verlängert werden.

7. Der Vertrag kann mit dreimonatiger Frist von jedem Vertragspartner gekündigt werden.

8. Nach einer Probezeit von sechs Monaten kann jeder Vertragspartner, unter Einhaltung einer einmonatigen Kündigungsfrist, den Vertrag kündigen.

9. Die Waren werden auf Kommissionsbasis verkauft. Die Firma ist jedoch bereit einen Teil der Verwaltungs- und Werbungskosten zu übernehmen. Der normale Kommissionssatz der Firma liegt für Auslandsvertreter bei 20% des Umsatzes. Diese Kommission ist zahlbar für alle vom Agenten oder seiner Mittelsperson gebuchten Aufträge und muss sämtliche Ausgaben einbeziehen die dem Agenten entstehen, vorausgesetzt, der Agent schickt der Firma eine genaue Auflistung aller Aufwendungen mit den dazugehörigen Quittungen. Die Kommission wird vierteljährlich ausbezahlt.

.../...

 **SIE SIND DRAN!**

- With _____ your letter of 9th September, I have _____ in confirming the franchise agreement authorising you to set up a branch of our company in Brazil. _____ are two copies of the franchise agreement. Please _____ copies and _____ one to me.

- The general conditions of the contract are as follows:
- The contract is _____ initially to 5 years, but may be _____ for a further year _____ an annual evaluation of your company's performance.
- Our representatives work _____ a commission _____
- Commission is _____ all orders.

Lösung auf Seite 143

14 DANKSCHREIBEN

FORMELLE DANKSCHREIBEN

Herr Müller ist sehr zufrieden mit seinem Englandaufenthalt und den Begegnungen mit Frau Johnson und George. Als er im Büro eine ruhige Minute hat, beschließt er Dankesbriefe zu schreiben. Der erste Brief geht an Frau Johnson, der zweite an George, den er außerdem etwas Wichtiges fragen möchte ...

---

(1) _____

(2) _____ for (3) _____ we had last Tuesday and
for (4) _____ . It was (5) _____ to visit your
company and become better acquainted with your business
operations.

I trust (6) _____ your order for the new products
(7) _____ , and look forward to (8) _____
between our two companies.

(9) _____

J. Müller

J Müller
Export Manager

⌐━━🔑 Brief 18: Lösung auf Seite 136

Helfen Sie ihm sein erstes Dankschreiben aufzusetzen:

(1) *Die Anrede:*
   Dear Angela
   Dear Madam
   Dear Mrs Johnson

(2) *Die Dankesformel:*
   I am interested in thanking you
   I must thank you
   I should like to thank you

(3) *Der Grund des Dankes:*
   the great time
   the fruitful meeting
   the good reunion

(4) *„Ihre Gastfreundschaft":*
   your excellent welcome
   your undivided attention
   your kind hospitality

(5) *Etwas bewerten:*
most interesting
great fun
a worthwhile experience

(6) *Den Eingang einer Bestellung erwarten:*
we shall shortly be receiving
you will not delay in sending
you have not forgotten about

(7) *An den Gegenstand des Geschäfts erinnern:*
I want you to buy
I showed you
we discussed during our meeting

(8) *Auf dauerhafte Zusammenarbeit hoffen:*
good relations
more meetings
renewed transactions

(9) *Die Grußformel:*
Yours faithfully
Yours sincerely
Regards

INFORMELLE DANKSCHREIBEN

In seinem Schreiben an George benutzt Jens Müller einen ganz anderen Stil. Hier ist sein vollständiger Brief:

Dear George

Many thanks for the very pleasant evening at the White Horse the other night. I haven't enjoyed myself so much for a long time and it was lovely to see you again; we ought to make it more of a regular event. Incidently, I found your friend Sarah particularly charming. I don't suppose you have her address do you?
Hope to see you again soon. Why don't you come and visit me in Berlin next time?

Best wishes

Jens

REDEWENDUNGEN

Dankesformeln
informell:

Many thanks for your help.	*Vielen Dank für deine Hilfe.*
Thank you for the lovely evening.	*Danke für den schönen Abend.*
Thanks very much for having us.	*Vielen Dank für deine Einladung.*
Thanks a lot for your letter.	*Herzlichen Dank für deinen Brief.*

formell:

I wanted / would like to thank you for your hospitality.	*Ich wollte / möchte Ihnen für Ihre Gastfreundschaft danken.*
Please accept our warmest thanks for… .	*Wir möchten uns ganz herzlich für … bedanken.*
It was most kind of you to offer us a reduction on the remainder of your stock.	*Es war sehr freundlich von Ihnen, uns auf den restlichen Lagerbestand einen Nachlass zu gewähren.*
We should like to express our gratitude / our sincere thanks for… .	*Wir möchten Ihnen unseren aufrichtigen Dank für … aussprechen.*
I am most grateful to you for all your help and hospitality during my stay in York.	*Ich bin Ihnen sehr dankbar für Ihre Hilfe und Gastfreundschaft während meines Aufenthalts in York.*
Thank you for your hospitality on the occasion of our meeting.	*Haben Sie Dank für Ihre Gastfreundschaft bei unserem Treffen.*

 ANMERKUNGEN

→ Beachten Sie den Gebrauch des Superlativs **most**, um etwas Positives hervorzuheben: **It was most interesting to visit…**, d. h.: Es war höchst / äußerst interessant … zu besuchen.

 **SIE SIND DRAN!**

• *Sie waren bei Freunden zum Abendessen eingeladen. Bedanken Sie sich schrift-lich bei ihnen für den schönen Abend (lovely evening) und das ausgezeichnete Essen (excellent meal).*

• Please _____ my warmest thanks _____ your kind _____ during my visit to Nairobi last week.

• I _____ you for the useful advice and the interesting documents you gave me _____ our last meeting.

Lösung auf Seite 144

15 ANGEBOTE UND EINLADUNGEN

FORMELLE EINLADUNG

Kurz nach seiner Rückkehr aus England erhält Herr Müller ein königliches Schreiben vom Buckingham Palace. Die Firma Luxiphon wird aufgefordert, sich im Rahmen einer Ausschreibung als offizieller Hoflieferant zu bewerben. Darüber hinaus wird Herr Müller zu einem Empfang eingeladen.

On Her Majesty's Service
Buckingham Palace
St James's Park, London

(1) _____

The administrators of Buckingham Palace (2) _____ to tender
(3) _____ to Her Majesty the Queen.

(4) _____ an invitation (5) _____ at the Palace, at which all current and potential suppliers will be present.

We look forward to (6) _____ .

(7) _____

R. Blue

R Blue
Administrator
Buckingham Palace

Enc

Brief 19: Lösung auf Seite 136

Her Majesty's Suppliers
request the pleasure of the company of
Mr J Müller
at a reception to be held at
Buckingham Palace
on Friday 20th June at 6 pm

Formal dress   RSVP

Vervollständigen Sie den Brief des Hofbeamten mit Hilfe nachfolgender Begriffe:

(1) *Die Anrede:*
Dear Sir / Madam
Dear Luxiphon
Dear Sir

(2) *Die Formulierung der Einladung:*
have pleasure in inviting you
are honoured to invite you
would like to invite you

(3) *Die Ankündigung der Ausschreibung:*
to be official supplier
for a position as official supplier
for a contract as official supplier

(4) *Auf eine Anlage hinweisen:*
We include herewith
Please find enclosed
Enclosed is

(5) *An einem Empfang teilnehmen:*
to attend a reception
to assist at a reception
to come to a party

(6) *Wir freuen uns auf „Ihre
baldige Antwort":*
your letter
seeing you
your early reply

(7) *Die Grußformel:*
Yours sincerely
Regards
Yours faithfully

INFORMELLE EINLADUNG

Herr Müller ist der Ansicht, dass diese kleine Reise nach England eine wunderbare Gelegenheit wäre, die bezaubernde junge Sarah Hampshire wiederzusehen, die er bei seinem Freund George kennengelernt hat. Er nimmt also seine schönste Feder zur Hand und beginnt mit seinem Brief …

Heinrich-Heine-Str. 85
10179 Berlin

Ms Sarah Hampshire   *3rd June 19…*
34 George Street
Birmingham

(1) _____

I have (2) _____ as (3) _____ in England again soon, for the week beginning 20th June, and (4) _____ spend an evening together. (5) _____ that new play at the Royal Theatre, followed, of course, by dinner ? (6) _____ which day (7) _____ , and I will ask my secretary (8) _____ .

I hope you will (9) _____ as I am very much looking forward to seeing you again.

(10) _____

Jens

⚷ Brief 20: Lösung auf Seite 136

Helfen Sie Herrn Müller dabei diesen sehr persönlichen Brief an Ms Hampshire zu schreiben:

(1) *Die Anrede:*
Dear Miss Hampshire
Dear Madam
Dear Sarah

(2) *Erste Kontaktaufnahme:*
intiated writing to you
taken the liberty of writing to you
considered writing to you

(3) *Sein Vorhaben ankündigen:*
I am due to be
I might be
I am probably

(4) *Vorsichtig anfragen:*
thought we might
was wondering if we could
wanted us to

(5) *Einen konkreten Vorschlag machen:*
What's about
How would you like to go to
And if we went to

(6) *Um Antwort bitten:*
Let me know
Tell me
Contact my secretary to say

(7) *„würde Ihnen am besten passen":*
would suit you best
fit in with your schedule
is fine by you

(8) *Die Aufgabe der Sekretärin:*
to occupy things
to get organised
to make the necessary reservations

(9) *„es einrichten können":*
come
be able to make it
be interested

(10) *Die Grußformel:*
Yours faithfully
Yours sincerely
Best wishes

 ## REDEWENDUNGEN

Formelle Einladungen

The chairman and directors have pleasure in inviting you to attend the company Christmas Party to be held at the Victoria Hotel, Knightsbridge, on Saturday, 20th December, at 8 o'clock.	*Der Vorsitzende und der Vorstand freuen sich, Sie am Samstag, dem 20. Dezember, um 20 Uhr zur Weihnachtsfeier der Firma ins Hotel Victoria, Knightsbridge einzuladen.*
Mr and Mrs Smith request the pleasure of the company of Mr and Mrs Jones at their daughter Jane's wedding reception to take place at... (place) on... (date) at... (time).	*Herr und Frau Smith geben sich die Ehre, Herrn und Frau Jones zur Hochzeit(sfeier) ihrer Tochter Jane am ... um ... in ... einzuladen.*

Informelle, private Einladungen

We are planning a small dinner party on... at... .

Wir möchten (euch) am ..., um ..., zu einem Abendessen im kleinen Kreis einladen.

We hope you will be able to come.

Wir hoffen, dass ihr kommen könnt.

We would be very pleased if you could have dinner with us on Friday evening.

Wir würden uns sehr freuen, wenn ihr Freitagabend zu uns zum Essen kommen könntet.

We wondered whether you would be interested in going to the opening night of... with us.

Wir haben uns überlegt, dass es dich vielleicht interessieren würde, mit uns zur Premiere von ... zu gehen.

I would like to invite you to accompany me on a trip to Russia next month.

Ich würde dich gerne einladen, mich nächsten Monat auf eine Russlandreise zu begleiten.

Would you be interested in coming with us to...?

Hättest du Lust mit uns nach ... zu kommen?

Zusätzliche Hinweise

formell:

formal dress	*Gesellschaftskleidung*
evening dress	*Abendkleidung*
fancy dress (US: costume)	*Verkleidung*
casual dress	*zwanglose / legere Kleidung*
informal / casual business attire	*legere Geschäftskleidung*
RSVP	*um Antwort wird gebeten*
Please reply before... .	*Bitte geben Sie bis ... Bescheid.*

informell:

Let me know which day would suit you best.

Sag mir bitte, welcher Tag dir am besten passt.

We do hope you can come.

Wir hoffen wirklich / sehr, dass du kommen kannst.

We are looking forward to seeing you.

Wir freuen uns darauf dich zu sehen.

Einladungen zu geschäftlichen Veranstaltungen

I should like to extend an invitation to you...

Hiermit möchte ich Sie einladen ...

to have lunch with our company staff on Thursday 9th December.

zu einem Mittagessen mit unseren Mitarbeitern am Donnerstag, den 9. Dezember.

to visit our premises.

unsere Geschäftsräume zu besuchen.

You are invited to attend a cocktail party after the conference.

Wir möchten Sie zu einer Cocktailparty einladen, die im Anschluss an die Konferenz stattfindet.

 **ANMERKUNGEN**

→ Beachten Sie, dass bei formellen, gedruckten Einladungen auf Anrede und Schlussformel verzichtet wird. Unten auf der Einladung können auch Einzelheiten erwähnt sein wie z. B. die erwünschte Kleidung oder die Bitte um Antwort. Hierfür benutzt man im Englischen übrigens die französische Abkürzung **RSVP** für „répondez s'il vous plaît".

→ Merken Sie sich die inhaltliche Reihenfolge auf einer Einladung:
- Wer lädt wen ein?
- Rahmen: **a reception, a banquet, a dinner…**
  (ein Empfang, ein Bankett, ein Abendessen)
- Ort: **to be held / to take place AT…** (findet … statt)
- Datum: **ON…** (am …)
- Uhrzeit: **AT…** (um …)
- Anlaß: **in honour of…** (zu Ehren von …)

 **SIE SIND DRAN!**

• The President of Europa Ltd _____ the _____ of your company _____ a luncheon to take _____ at the York Hotel, Chelsea _____ Thursday, 5th March, _____ 1 o'clock, in _____ of his retirement.

• We are going to the theatre next week with a few friends and _____ _____ if you _____ come.

• Mr and Mrs Simpson request the _____ of your _____ at a banquet _____ held _____ the Ritz Hotel, on Friday 21 April, _____ 6 pm.

• We _____ some friends over _____ lunch next Sunday. We would be _____ if you _____ join us.

• I wondered _____ you would be interested _____ going _____ a museum next week. Let me know whether you _____ come.

Lösung auf Seite 144

16 EINLADUNGEN BEANTWORTEN

FORMELLE ANTWORTEN

Herr Müller freut sich sehr über die Einladung aus dem Buckingham Palace und beschließt sofort zuzusagen. Er fasst zwei verschiedene Antwortschreiben ab, da es sich um zwei unterschiedliche Anlässe handelt: die Ausschreibung und den Empfang.

                                                           3rd June 19...

(1) _____

(2) _____ of 1st June (3) _____ your invitation
(4) _____ as official supplier to Her Majesty the Queen.

(5) _____ receiving further (6) _____
regarding the tender procedure.

(7) _____

J. Müller

J Müller
Export Manager

⚷ Brief 21: Lösung auf Seite 137

Dear Sir

Mr Müller (8) _____ Her Majesty's Suppliers
(9) _____ to the reception at Buckingham Palace on
Friday 20th June which (10) _____ .

Yours faithfully

J. Müller

J Müller
Export Manager
Luxiphon

⚷ Brief 22: Lösung auf Seite 137

Helfen Sie ihm die beiden Briefe zu verfassen und wählen Sie den jeweils passenden Begriff:

Zusage zur Ausschreibung

(1) *Die Anrede:*
Dear Mr Blue
Dear Madam
To whom it may concern

(2) *Sich auf ein Schreiben beziehen:*
In reply to your letter
Regarding your correspondence
About your invitation

(3) *Die Einladung annehmen:*
we are glad to accept
we have pleasure in accepting
we must accept

(4) *An der Ausschreibung teilnehmen:*
to apply for a position
to work
to tender for a contract

(5) *Um zusätzliche Informationen bitten:*
We are keen on
We look forward to
We would be interested in

(6) *„schriftliches Material":*
news
brochures
instructions and documentation

(7) *Die Grußformel:*
Yours sincerely
Regards
Yours faithfully

Zusage zum Empfang

(8) *Sich für die Einladung bedanken:*
is grateful to
would like to express his
   warmest thanks to
thanks

(9) *An den Anlass erinnern:*
for having invited him
for sending him an invitation
for their kind invitation

(10) *Die Einladung annehmen:*
he has much pleasure in accepting
he is pleased to accept
he accepts

INFORMELLE ANTWORTEN

Herr Müller erhält eine Antwort von Sarah Hampshire, die er ins Theater eingeladen hatte.

---

(1) _____

(2) _____ *for the invitation. (3)* _____ *to
go to the theatre with you. The best day for me would be Monday 23rd June.
(4)* _____ *to see you again!*

(5) _____

Sarah

O—— Brief 23: Lösung auf Seite 137

Vervollständigen Sie ihren Brief mit Hilfe folgender Begriffe:

(1) *Die Anrede:*
   Dear Jens
   Dear Sir
   Dear Mr Müller

(2) *Sich bedanken:*
   Thanks
   Please accept my sincerest thanks
   I should like to express my gratitude

(3) *Die Einladung annehmen:*
   I have pleasure in accepting
   I should be honoured
   I would be delighted

(4) *Vorfreude ausdrücken:*
   We look forward
   It will be a pleasure
   I am keen

(5) *Die Grußformel:*
   Best wishes
   Yours faithfully
   Yours sincerely

 **REDEWENDUNGEN**

Sich für eine Einladung bedanken
formell:

Mr and Mrs John Smith thank Mr and Mrs David Smythe for their kind invitation to dinner.
Thank you for your kind invitation to the conference.

Wir bedanken uns herzlich bei Ihnen für die freundliche Einladung zum Abendessen. (besonders förmlich)
Wir bedanken uns für Ihre freundliche Einladung zur Teilnahme an der Konferenz.

informell:

Thanks a lot for the invitation.
Many thanks for the invitation to lunch.

Vielen Dank für die Einladung.
Vielen Dank für die Einladung zum Mittagessen.

Eine Einladung annehmen
formell:

… which they / we / I have much pleasure in accepting.
… which I / we should / would be delighted to accept.

… die sie / wir / ich gern annehme(n).

… die ich / wir sehr gern annehme(n) / annehmen würde(n).

informell:

I would love to come.
I would be delighted to join you on Thursday.

Ich komme sehr gern.
Ich würde mich sehr freuen am Donnerstag dabei zu sein.

Eine Einladung absagen
formell:

… which they are regretfully unable to accept owing to a prior engagement.
… which he is unfortunately unable to attend owing to… .
… which I must unfortunately decline as I shall be out of the country on 5th September.

… der sie leider wegen einer anderweitigen Verpflichtung nicht nachkommen können.
… an dem / der er leider wegen … nicht teilnehmen kann.
… den / die / das ich leider absagen muss, da ich am 5. September im Ausland bin.

informell:

I am afraid I won't be able to make it on Saturday as I already have something on.

Leider kann ich am Samstag nicht kommen, da ich schon etwas vorhabe.

Unfortunately I will be out of town on the 27th and therefore will not be able to attend the conference.	*Bedauerlicherweise bin ich am 27. nicht in der Stadt und werde deshalb nicht an der Konferenz teilnehmen können.*

ANMERKUNGEN

→ Merken Sie sich folgende Präpositionen, die ähnlich wie im Deutschen verwendet werden:
your invitation TO the dinner / banquet / reception AT Bicton Hall
Aber ganz anders als im Deutschen:
we have much pleasure IN accepting...

SIE SIND DRAN!

formell:
• Mr and Mrs Jones _____ Mr and Mrs Cavendish _____.
their _____ invitation _____ dinner, which they are
regretfully _____ to accept _____ to a prior engagement.

informell:
• _____ for the invitation _____ dinner.
I _____ I won't _____ to make it as I am going
on holiday next week.

• Thank _____ very much _____ to spend a
weekend in Glasgow. We _____ delighted to _____ .

⟀ Lösung auf Seite 144

17 GESCHÄFTLICHE MITTEILUNGEN

Herr Müller ist sehr stolz: Luxiphon wurde zum offiziellen Lieferanten der Königin von England bestimmt. Hiervon möchte er auf jeden Fall die Kundschaft in Kenntnis setzen!

LUXI PHON
Magdeburger Straße 250 • 10785 Berlin

Purchasing Department
Barnes & Sons
100 Greyson Gardens
London W1 SQ2   2nd July 19...

(1) _____

(2) _____ that our company has recently been accepted as official supplier to Her Majesty the Queen.

This contract (3) _____ the excellent quality and service (4) _____ our customers. To mark the event we are offering special prices on our Mars and Princess ranges if (5) _____ before 1st August. We are sending you our latest catalogue (6) _____ _____ .

We look forward to maintaining the special relationship we have with our customers and to continuing to (7) _____ the prompt service and quality products (8) _____ .

(9) _____

J. Müller

J Müller
Export Manager

⚷ Brief 24: Lösung auf Seite 137

Helfen Sie ihm, seine Mailing-Aktion vorzubereiten:

(1) *Die Anrede:*
Dear Sir
Dear Sir / Madam
Dear Customer

(2) *Eine Nachricht ankündigen:*
We are announcing
We have pleasure in announcing
This is just to let you know

(3) *Eine Begründung anführen:*
is due to the fact that
was rewarded for
comes as a reward for

(4) *„wir sind immer bemüht, ...*
anzubieten":
we give
we always strive to offer
we are offering

(5) *„(wenn) Sie Ihre Bestellung*
aufgeben":
you place your order
you give your order
you pass your order

(6) *„mit getrennter Post":*
enclosed
soon
under separate cover

(7) *Die Kundschaft beliefern:*
give them
furnish them with
provide them with

(8) *Die Gewohnheiten der Kunden*
ansprechen:
they are accustomed to
which they are accustomed
they want

(9) *Die Grußformel:*
Best wishes
Yours faithfully
Yours sincerely

 REDEWENDUNGEN

Ein Ereignis ankündigen

We are writing to inform you that
Mr Hampshire will be retiring as
Chairman of the Board in June.

You will be interested to know that
we have just introduced / brought
out our new range of DIY products.
We have pleasure in announcing
the opening of our new High Street
branch.

Hiermit informieren wir Sie, dass
Herr Hampshire im Juni aus seiner
Position als Vorstandsvorsitzender
ausscheiden wird.
Es wird Sie interessieren, dass wir gerade
unser neuestes Sortiment an Heimwer-
kerprodukten herausgebracht haben.
Wir freuen uns, die Eröffnung unserer
neuen Zweigstelle im Stadtzentrum
bekannt geben zu können.

We have pleasure in informing / notifying you of the recent merger of our company with Matsita Computers Ltd.

Wir freuen uns, Ihnen die kürzlich vollzogene Fusion unserer Firma mit Matsita Computers mitteilen zu können.

May we draw your attention to the long-awaited arrival of our new "Fun Pens"?

Wir möchten Sie darauf aufmerksam machen, dass unsere lang erwarteten „Fun"-Schreiber jetzt eingetroffen sind.

We are pleased to be able to give you details of our brand-new model of vacuum cleaner.

Wir freuen uns, Sie in allen Einzelheiten über unser allerneuestes Staubsaugermodell informieren zu können.

We are delighted to introduce to you our brand-new range of office furniture.

Wir freuen uns sehr, Ihnen unsere allerneueste Büromöbelserie vorstellen zu können.

Auf ein Sonderangebot aufmerksam machen

To mark the event we are offering... special prices on our... (product).

Zu diesem Anlass bieten wir ... Sonderpreise für unser(e) ... .

a special discount for all orders exceeding £500.

einen Sonderrabatt auf alle Bestellungen über £500.

a discount of 3% if you place your order before 1st May.

einen Rabatt von 3%, wenn Sie Ihre Bestellung vor dem 1. Mai aufgeben.

To mark the occasion we are making a special offer of a free gift with every order.

Aus diesem Anlass erhalten Sie gratis zu jeder Bestellung ein Geschenk.

Vorteile und Besonderheiten hervorheben

As a result of this merger we are able to offer you a much wider range of products and significant price reductions.

Infolge dieser Fusion können wir Ihnen eine viel breitere Produktpalette und beträchtliche Preisnachlässe gewähren.

You will find this new version of the... (product) even more accurate / efficient / attractive / economical / user-friendly / reliable.

Sie werden feststellen, dass diese neue Variante von ... (Produkt) sogar noch genauer / leistungsfähiger / attraktiver / wirtschaftlicher / anwenderfreundlicher / zuverlässiger ist.

Our new branch has the added advantage of being situated right in the heart of the business district.

Unsere neue Zweigstelle bietet zusätzlich den Vorteil, dass sie mitten im Geschäftsviertel liegt.

Our products are reputed for their ingenious design, high quality, and competitive prices.

Unsere Produkte sind für ihr originelles Design, ihre hohe Qualität und konkurrenzfähige Preise bekannt.

Danksagungen

It came to my notice recently that, after fifteen years doing business

Kürzlich stellte ich fest, dass Ihre Firma nach 15-jähriger geschäftlicher

together, your company is one of our oldest customers. I would like to take this opportunity of thanking you for your regular patronage. We also very much appreciate your continued contribution to the prosperity of our business through your recommendations to potential customers.	*Zusammenarbeit einer unserer ältesten Kunden ist. Ich möchte diese Gelegenheit nutzen um Ihnen für Ihre langjährige Treue zu danken. Auch wissen wir es sehr zu schätzen, dass Sie durch die Weiterempfehlung an potenzielle neue Kunden zur Prosperität unserer Firma beigetragen haben.*

 ## ANMERKUNGEN

→ **We are offering** wird vorzugsweise verwendet wenn es sich um ein zeitlich begrenztes Angebot handelt, **we offer**, wenn das Produkt immer zur Angebotspalette gehört.

→ Beachten Sie, dass die unterschiedliche Position der Präposition **to** in den nachfolgenden Beispielen einen Unterschied in der Sprachebene anzeigt:
formell = **TO which they are accustomed**
informell = **which they are accustomed TO**

 ## SIE SIND DRAN!

• You will be _____ that we have just brought out a new _____ of hi-fi equipment. To _____ the occasion, we _____ a discount on all orders _____ £2000. We _____ our latest catalogue _____ separate cover.

• We _____ in announcing the merger of _____ with United Motors Ltd. As _____ of this merger we _____ to offer a much wider _____ of cars at reduced _____ .

• To mark the opening of _____ factory _____ New Malden, we _____ 5% off list-price if _____ your order within the next month.

• You _____ interested to know that we have recently brought _____ our _____ -new selection _____ ozone-friendly hairsprays. You _____ find this version _____ the hairspray _____ economical and easy to use.

Lösung auf Seite 144

18 PERSÖNLICHE KORRESPONDENZ

Herr Müller erfährt, dass seine Ansprechpartnerin bei Electron, Angela Johnson, kürzlich zur Europabeauftragten ihrer Firma befördert wurde. Er schickt ihr Glückwünsche.

LUXI PHON
Magdeburger Straße 250 • 10785 Berlin

Mrs A Johnson
Electron Ltd
25 St James Street
Birmingham B25 8HO   18th September 19...

(1) _____

(2) _____ to learn that you (3) _____ Regional Manager for Europe. (4) _____ in your new post, for which I am sure you have just (5) _____ and experience.

My colleagues (6) _____ our warmest congratulations, and we look forward to (7) _____ .

(8) _____

Jens Müller

Jens Müller

Brief 25: Lösung auf Seite 137

Helfen Sie ihm seine Glückwünsche in die richtige schriftliche Form zu bringen:

(1) *Die Anrede:*
   Dear Madam
   Dear Angela
   To whom it may concern

(2) *Welche Zeitform ist richtig?*
   I was delighted
   I have been delighted
   I would be delighted

(3) „ernannt worden sind":
    have become
    have been positioned
    have been appointed

(4) *Erfolg wünschen:*
    I hope you will be successful
    May I wish you every success
    May your success be great

(5) *Kompetenz anerkennen:*
    the good qualities
    the right qualities
    the best qualities

(6) *Gemeinsame Wünsche schicken:*
    send you
    join me in wishing you
    join me in sending you

(7) *"unsere langjährige Zusammen-
    arbeit fortzusetzen":*
    continuing our long association
    your continued custom
    your next order

(8) *Die Grußformel:*
    Yours faithfully
    With best wishes
    Yours sincerely

 REDEWENDUNGEN

Glückwünsche aussprechen

I am writing to send you my warmest congratulations on your recent promotion to… (post).

Hiermit möchte ich Ihnen meine herz-lichsten Glückwünsche zu Ihrer kürz-lichen Beförderung zum / zur … (Stelle) übermitteln.

We were pleased to hear of your appointment to the presidency of the company, and wish you every success in managing the affairs of such a flourishing enterprise.

Wir haben uns gefreut zu hören, dass Sie in den Vorstand der Firma berufen wurden, und wünschen Ihnen allen erdenklichen Erfolg bei der Leitung solch eines florierenden Unternehmens.

We have just heard the good news. Many congratulations from all of us here to you and your wife / hus-band on the birth of your baby boy / girl.

Wir haben soeben von dem freudigen Ereignis gehört. Ihnen und Ihrer Frau / Ihrem Mann die herzlichsten Glück-wünsche von uns allen zur Geburt Ihres kleinen Jungen / Ihrer kleinen Tochter.

Please accept our heartiest congratulations.

Wir senden Ihnen unsere herzlichsten Glückwünsche.

We should like to send you our con-gratulations on the occasion of your golden wedding anniversary / your company's hundredth anniversary.

Wir möchten Ihnen zu Ihrer Goldenen Hochzeit / zum 100jährigen Bestehen Ihrer Firma unsere Glückwünsche übermitteln.

Gute Wünsche zum Jahreswechsel

We send you and your family our very best wishes for a happy Christmas and a prosperous New Year.

Wir wünschen Ihnen und Ihrer Familie ein frohes Weihnachtsfest und ein glückliches neues Jahr.

Best wishes for Christmas and the New Year.

Frohe Weihnachten und ein glückliches neues Jahr.

We would like to take this opportunity of thanking our customers for their continued patronage and of sending them our best wishes for Christmas and the New Year.

Bei dieser Gelegenheit möchten wir all unseren Kunden für Ihre Treue danken und Ihnen ein schönes Weihnachtsfest und alles Gute fürs neue Jahr wünschen.

Willkommensgrüße

Welcome to Singapore. I hope you have found a suitable house and are settling in well. Should you be in need of anything, please do not hesitate to contact me at the above address.

Willkommen in Singapur. Ich hoffe, Sie haben ein geeignetes Haus gefunden und leben sich gut ein. Sollten Sie irgendetwas benötigen, so zögern Sie bitte nicht, mich unter der obigen Adresse zu kontaktieren.

Kondolenzschreiben

May I offer you my sincere condolences? If there is anything I can do to help, please do not hesitate to let me know.

Ich möchte Ihnen mein aufrichtiges Beileid ausdrücken. Wenn ich irgendetwas für Sie tun kann, so lassen Sie es mich bitte sofort wissen.

I was deeply distressed to hear of the sudden death of Mr Hargreaves, whom we knew as an outstanding member of your staff and a good friend. All of us at Sunbeam Associates would like to convey our sincere sympathy to his family and friends.

Die Nachricht von dem plötzlichen Tod von Herrn Hargreaves, den wir alle als hervorragenden Mitarbeiter Ihres Teams und als guten Freund kannten, hat mich tief erschüttert. Wir alle von Sunbeam Associates möchten seiner Familie und seinen Freunden unser tiefstes Mitgefühl ausdrücken.

We were deeply sorry to hear about Janet's tragic death. It is a great loss to all who knew her. Would you be so kind as to pass on our condolences to her husband and family.

Die Nachricht von Janets tragischem Tod hat uns mit tiefer Trauer erfüllt. Er bedeutet einen großen Verlust für alle, die sie kannten. Bitte seien Sie so freundlich, ihrem Mann und ihrer Familie unser Beileid zu übermitteln.

You have the deepest sympathy of everyone on our staff.

Seien Sie des tiefsten Mitgefühls unserer gesamten Belegschaft versichert.

Genesungswünsche

I was sorry to hear that you have been taken ill. I trust that it is nothing too serious. In the meantime, please accept my very best wishes for a complete and speedy recovery.

Es tat mir leid zu erfahren, dass Sie krank geworden sind. Ich hoffe, es ist nichts allzu Ernstes, und wünsche Ihnen zwischenzeitlich, dass Sie sich schnell und vollständig erholen.

We were all very sorry to hear about your accident. However, we were relieved to learn that you are over the worst and are likely to be back at the office next month. In the meantime, we all send our best wishes for a speedy recovery.

Es tat uns allen sehr leid, von Ihrem Unfall zu erfahren. Wir waren jedoch sehr erleichtert zu hören, dass Sie das Schlimmste überstanden haben und wahrscheinlich (bereits) nächsten Monat wieder im Büro sein werden. Fürs Erste senden wir Ihnen alle unsere besten Wünsche für eine schnelle Genesung.

I trust you are feeling better, and send you my best wishes for a speedy recovery.

Ich hoffe es geht Ihnen besser und wünsche Ihnen baldige Genesung.

We were glad to hear that you are making good progress.

Wir freuten uns zu erfahren, dass Sie gute Fortschritte machen.

 ANMERKUNGEN

→ Merken Sie sich, dass **to be appointed** dem deutschen „ernannt werden" entspricht, **appointment** dagegen hat mehrere Bedeutungen: einerseits kann es „Termin" oder „Verabredung" heißen, andererseits aber auch „Ernennung" oder „Anstellung".

→ Beachten Sie auch, dass die Redewendung „(eine Neuigkeit) erfahren" im Englischen entweder durch **to learn** oder durch **to hear** ausgedrückt werden kann: **I was sorry to learn / hear that... .**

SIE SIND DRAN!

- I was _____ to _____ that you have been taken ill. Please _____ my very best wishes for _____ recovery.

- We were deeply sorry to hear _____ Henry's tragic death. Please _____ our condolences _____ his wife and family.

- It came to my notice recently _____ after 15 years _____ business together, your company _____ become one of _____ oldest customers. I _____ to take the opportunity of _____ you for _____ regular patronage.

- I _____ to learn _____ you have been appointed Sales Manager. _____ wish you _____ in your _____ post. With _____ wishes.

Lösung auf Seite 144 / 145

19 MÄNGEL UND REKLAMATIONEN

Herr Müller erhält von einem Kunden eine Schadensmeldung wegen defekter Ware, die kürzlich von Luxiphon verschickt wurde. Glücklicherweise ist es ein höflicher Brief …

Himes Associates   **Purchasing Department**
251 Northern Road
Manchester • England

The Export Manager
Luxiphon
Magdeburger Str. 250
10785 Berlin   3rd October 19…

Ref: GB / SD

Dear Mr Müller,

(1) _____ this morning of our order no. 671B.
(2) _____ , some of the crates were damaged, and on unpacking them we found a number of breakages. We would suggest this is due
either to (3) _____ or to an accident in transit.
As sale was on a cif basis, we presume (4) _____ from the
carrier. We estimate the value of the damage at around £2,500.
We will, of course, be keeping the damaged crates and their contents
(5) _____ . (6) _____ the guarantee, we should
be most grateful if you would (7) _____ for the damaged items.
A list of these is enclosed.
We must ask you to (8) _____ as this delay is
(9) _____ .
We look forward to an early reply.

Yours sincerely

G. Braun

G Brown
Purchasing Department

○══ Brief 26: Lösung auf Seite 138

Vervollständigen Sie die Reklamation mit Hilfe folgender Begriffe:

(1) *Den Erhalt der Lieferung bestätigen:*
   We took delivery
   We were delivered
   We had received delivery

(2) *Sein Bedauern ausdrücken:*
   We regret that
   We were sorry that
   Regrettably

(3) *Eine Erklärung anbieten:*
   your having packed them wrongly
   a serious error committed by
     the packers
   inadequate packing

(4) *Eine Schadensregulierung
   vorschlagen:*
   you will be getting compensation
   you will be claiming compensation
   you would insist on compensation

(5) *Eine Schadensinspektion
   vorschlagen:*
   as evidence
   for inspection
   as a control

(6) *An die Garantie erinnern:*
   As we agreed when signing
   As you are bound by
   Under the terms of

(7) *Schadensersatz verlangen:*
   make sure we get replacements
   send a replacement
   give us money

(8) *Um eine schnelle Abwicklung
   bitten:*
   hurry up
   get it done quickly
   attend to the matter with the utmost
     urgency

(9) *Unannehmlichkeiten ansprechen:*
   a real nuisance to us
   causing us great inconvenience
   a problem

 REDEWENDUNGEN

Wegen einer Lieferverzögerung reklamieren

The goods we ordered on 5th January (order no. GH550) have not yet arrived.	*Die Ware, die wir am 5. Januar bestellt haben (Bestell-Nr. GH550), ist noch nicht eingetroffen.*
We have not yet received our order no. 66 which we understood was shipped on 6th March.	*Wir haben die bestellte Ware (Bestell-Nr. 66) noch nicht erhalten, von der wir annahmen, sie sei am 6. März verschickt worden.*
We regret to inform you that our order no. GH550, which should have been delivered on 1st April, is now considerably overdue.	*Leider müssen wir Ihnen mitteilen, dass sich die Lieferung (Bestell-Nr. GH550), die am 1. April hätte bei uns eingehen sollen, erheblich verspätet hat.*

Please look into the non-delivery of the 500 desklamps which we ordered on November 25th.	*Bitte prüfen Sie, warum die 500 Schreibtischlampen, die wir am 25. November bestellt haben, noch nicht geliefert wurden.*
We still have not received the goods we ordered on March 12th. As this order was placed on condition that we received the consignment before 15th April, we will be obliged to take our custom elsewhere.	*Wir haben die am 12. März bestellte Ware immer noch nicht erhalten. Da diese Bestellung unter der Bedingung erfolgte, dass wir die Lieferung vor dem 15. April erhalten würden, sehen wir uns gezwungen unsere Ware von anderer Stelle zu beziehen.*

Schäden nach Auslieferung der Ware melden

We took delivery on 2nd December of our order no. 51. However, several crates were missing, and others had been damaged.	*Am 2. Dezember erhielten wir Ihre Lieferung (Bestell-Nr. 51). Jedoch fehlten einige Kisten und andere waren defekt.*
Upon receipt of our order no. 777 we found that the boxes had been broken open and some items removed.	*Bei Entgegennahme Ihrer Lieferung (Bestell-Nr. 777) stellten wir fest, dass die Kisten aufgebrochen und einige Teile entfernt worden waren.*
Our consignment of… was stolen in transit.	*Der / Die / Das von uns bestellte(n) … wurde(n) während des Transports gestohlen.*
We regret to report that our consignment of… was delivered this morning in an unsatisfactory condition. A detailed list of the damaged items is enclosed.	*Wir müssen Ihnen leider mitteilen, dass der / die / das von uns bestellte[n] … uns heute morgen in mangelhaftem Zustand zugestellt wurde(n). Eine detaillierte Aufstellung aller beschädigten Teile liegt bei.*

Eine zweite Reklamation / Beschwerde formulieren
(mit größerem Nachdruck)

I am extremely concerned at your failure to deliver the consignment of spare parts promised for March 20th.	*Ich bin sehr darüber besorgt, dass Sie nicht in der Lage sind, die für den 20. März zugesicherte Ersatzteillieferung vorzunehmen.*
I feel I should point out that this is not the first time we have had to complain for a similar reason, and although I appreciate there may be a valid explanation for the delay, I cannot allow our production schedules to be disrupted.	*Ich möchte betonen, dass dies nicht das erste Mal ist, dass wir Grund zu einer ähnlichen Beschwerde haben. Obwohl es möglicherweise eine stichhaltige Erklärung für diese Verzögerung gibt, kann ich es nicht zulassen, dass dadurch unser Produktionsplan durcheinander gebracht wird.*

I would be reluctant to have to change suppliers in the hope of better service.

Ich würde nur ungern in der Hoffnung auf einen besseren Service zu einem anderen Anbieter überwechseln.

The disruption to our production caused by your company's inefficiency has been most serious and we have been forced to supply our needs from another manufacturer at considerable inconvenience.

Die aufgrund der Inkompetenz Ihrer Firma eingetretene Produktionsunterbrechung hat uns in ernste Schwierigkeiten gebracht. Wir sind deshalb, auch wenn uns dies größte Unannehmlichkeiten verursacht, gezwungen, unseren Bedarf bei einem anderen Lieferanten zu decken.

Die infolge der Schadensfeststellung unternommenen Schritte

We have marked the delivery slip accordingly.

Wir haben eine entsprechende Notiz auf dem Lieferschein vermerkt.

We have reported the damage to the carriers and will be keeping the damaged crates and their contents for inspection.

Wir haben dem Spediteur den Schaden gemeldet und behalten vorläufig die defekten Kisten und ihren Inhalt zwecks Inspektion.

We have had a survey of the damage carried out. A copy of the report has been sent to our insurance company.

Wir haben eine Schadensaufnahme machen lassen. Eine Kopie des Gutachtens wurde unserer Versicherung zugeschickt.

Erklärungen geben

Delivery was delayed as the goods were sent to our previous address.

Die Auslieferung hat sich verzögert, weil die Ware an unsere alte Adresse geschickt wurde.

The goods were damaged due to inadequate packing.

Die Waren wurden wegen unsachgemäßer Verpackung beschädigt.

The consignment was incorrectly labelled.

Der Auftrag war falsch beschriftet.

Lösungen anbieten

We should be grateful if you would arrange for replacements of the following articles to be sent as soon as possible.

Wir wären Ihnen dankbar, wenn Sie sobald wie möglich für eine Ersatzlieferung folgender Artikel sorgen könnten.

Please arrange for reimbursement of the value of the damaged goods.

Bitte sorgen Sie für die Rückerstattung des Wertes der beschädigten Ware.

We are returning the articles in question. Please credit us with the value of the returned goods.

Wir schicken die betreffenden Artikel zurück. Bitte schreiben Sie uns den Wert der zurückgegebenen Waren gut.

We are prepared to keep these unsuitable goods, but at a substantially reduced price.

If you were to deduct the sum of £50 from our next order, we would consider the matter closed.

Wir sind bereit, diese, für uns ungeeignete Ware zu behalten, jedoch nur zu einem großzügig reduzierten Preis.

Wenn Sie bereit sind, uns bei unserer nächsten Bestellung £50 zu erlassen, betrachten wir die Angelegenheit als erledigt.

Auf einen Fehler bei der Zusammenstellung des Auftrags hinweisen

We would like to draw your attention to the fact that, of the items supplied, one lot was of the wrong colour and another was of a larger size than ordered. We are returning both lots and would ask you to send replacements as soon as possible.

We were surprised to find that the complete order was not delivered. Would you please look into this for us?

Wir möchten Sie darauf hinweisen, dass bei der gelieferten Ware eine Partie die falsche Farbe hatte und eine andere eine größere Größe als bestellt.
Wir senden beide Partien zurück und bitten Sie um schnellstmöglichen Ersatz.

Wir waren überrascht, dass nicht die vollständige Ware geliefert wurde.
Wir bitten Sie, sich um die Angelegenheit zu kümmern.

Eine Rechnung zurückweisen

We found, on checking your invoice no. 900, that our figures do not tally with yours.

It appears that in invoice no. 88 you have failed to credit us with the agreed discount of 2%.

We notice that you have charged for extra insurance coverage which was not stipulated in the original agreement.

We should like to query the charge for packing which seems unusually high.

We have noticed a number of discrepancies in your latest invoice. We would be grateful if you would look into this and forward us a modified invoice.

Bei der Prüfung Ihrer Rechnung Nr. 900 stellten wir fest, dass Ihre Zahlen nicht mit unseren übereinstimmen.

Es scheint, dass Sie es in Rechnung Nr. 88 versäumt haben, uns die zugesagten 2% Nachlass zu gewähren.

Wir stellen fest, dass Sie uns zusätzliche Versicherungskosten berechnen, die im Originalvertrag nicht abgesprochen waren.

Wir möchten um eine Erklärung bezüglich der Verpackungsgebühren bitten, die uns ungewöhnlich hoch erscheinen.

In Ihrer letzten Rechnung stießen wir auf einige Ungereimtheiten.
Wir wären Ihnen dankbar, wenn Sie sie überprüfen und uns eine korrigierte Rechnung schicken könnten.

Sich über schlechten Service beschweren

I regret to have to complain about the appalling service I received from one of your maintenance engineers last week. Not only did he arrive three hours late, but he failed to clean up after repairing the machine and was exceedingly impolite.

Ich bedaure es, mich über den miserablen Service einer Ihrer Wartungsingenieure beschweren zu müssen, der mich letzte Woche aufsuchte. Er erschien nicht nur drei Stunden zu spät, sondern war auch nicht bereit, die Maschine sauber zu machen, die er repariert hatte. Außerdem war er noch extrem unhöflich.

 ## ANMERKUNGEN

→ Bei einer Reklamation ist es angebracht folgende Schritte einzuhalten:
* Genau erklären, worum es sich handelt: **I am writing with reference to… . / Yesterday we received our order no. … .**
* Das Problem darlegen und eine mögliche Erklärung anbieten.
* Eine Lösung vorschlagen (Kostenerstattung, Ersatz, etc.).

→ Beachten Sie den Gebrauch von **under** in der Redewendung **under the terms of the contract**, die hier die gleiche Bedeutung hat wie **according to**.

 ## SIE SIND DRAN!

* We _____ delivery yesterday _____ our order no. 45K. We found on _____ the crates that several items were missing. A list of the missing articles is _____ . Please arrange for _____ of these goods to _____ as soon as possible.

* We _____ to inform you that our order no. 89 _____ not arrived. This _____ is causing us great _____ _____ as we have a very tight production _____ .

* I am extremely _____ at your repeated failure to _____ our consignments on time. If there is no improvement I am _____ we shall have to take our custom elsewhere.

* I _____ to your invoice no. 789, in which we have noticed a number of _____ . I should _____ you would look into this and _____ us a _____ invoice.

Lösung auf Seite 145

20 REKLAMATIONEN BEANTWORTEN

Herr Müller beantwortet die Reklamation, die ihm Herr Graham Brown geschickt hat.

LUXI PHON
Magdeburger Straße 250 · 10785 Berlin

Mr G Brown
Himes Associates
251 Northern Road
Manchester – England   15th October 19…

Your ref: GB / SD
Our ref: JM / SG

(1) _____

We were (2) _____ your letter of October 3rd that the consignment of telephones ordered from us was (3) _____ .
We (4) _____ this has caused you.
Upon investigation, we have ascertained that the consignment was
packed (5) _____ , which (6) _____ is more
than adequate for a journey of the kind undertaken. Any damage
(7) _____ , however, is the responsibility of the carrier, and we
have (8) _____ our insurance company, who will be contacting
you shortly.
I have asked one of our agents to arrange to call at your
(9) _____ to inspect the damage. In the meantime, a
replacement for the damaged articles was despatched today.
Once again, (10) _____ for the inconvenience caused, and
trust that you will find the replacements (11) _____ .

Yours sincerely

J. Müller

J Müller
Export Manager

Brief 27: Lösung auf Seite 138

Helfen Sie ihm mit Hilfe folgender Begriffe eine Entschuldigung zu formulieren:

(1) *Die Anrede:*
Dear Sir
Dear Graham
Dear Mr Brown

(2) *Sorge ausdrücken:*
concerned to learn from
interested to hear in
very angry to read in

(3) *Auf eine beschädigte Lieferung hinweisen:*
in a bad way when it arrived
damaged on arrival
broken in transit

(4) *Sein Bedauern ausdrücken:*
are very sorry that the problems
send our most humble apologies for the trouble
very much regret the inconvenience

(5) *„in der üblichen Weise":*
in the usual manner
as usual
usually

(6) *„gemäß unserer Erfahrung":*
as far as we are concerned
as far as we know
in our experience

(7) *Welche Zeitform ist richtig?*
occurring in transit
to occur in transit
that will occur in transit

(8) *Eine Angelegenheit weiterleiten:*
transferred to
handed the matter over to
given the affair to

(9) *„die Geschäftsräume / das Anwesen":*
house
factory
premises

(10) *Sich entschuldigen:*
please accept our most humble apologies
sorry
we apologize

(11) *Für die Zufriedenheit des Kunden garantieren:*
fine by you
OK
to your entire satisfaction

 REDEWENDUNGEN

Den Erhalt einer Reklamation bestätigen

We have received your letter of... telling us that... .

Wir haben Ihren Brief / Ihr Schreiben vom ... erhalten, in dem Sie uns mitteilen, dass ... .

We were concerned to learn from your letter of... that... .

Wir waren besorgt, als wir aus Ihrem Brief vom ... erfuhren, dass ... .

Thank you for your letter of… informing us that… .
We were sorry to hear that… .

Vielen Dank für Ihren Brief vom …, der uns davon in Kenntnis setzte, dass … .
Es tat uns leid erfahren zu müssen, dass … .

Lieferverzögerungen erklären

We are sorry we have not yet been able to deliver your order no. 543. This is due to industrial action at our factory in Wolverhampton. Delivery will take place as soon as the strike is over.

Wir bedauern, dass wir die, von Ihnen bestellte Ware (Bestell-Nr. 543), wegen eines Arbeitskampfes in unserer Fabrik in Wolverhampton noch nicht liefern konnten. Sobald der Streik beendet ist, wird die Lieferung erfolgen.

We apologize for the delay, but our warehouse was recently damaged by fire. We will be able to deliver in three weeks' time.

Wir entschuldigen uns für die Verzögerung, aber unser Lager wurde kürzlich durch ein Feuer beschädigt. Wir werden in drei Wochen liefern können.

Please accept our sincere apologies for this delay and the trouble it has caused you. We have arranged for a replacement to be dispatched immediately.

Wir bitten Sie sehr, die Verzögerung und die Schwierigkeiten, die Ihnen dadurch entstanden sind, zu entschuldigen. Wir lassen Ihnen umgehend Ersatzware zugehen.

The delay is due to customs complications which are holding up all shipments to the United States. We are doing everything in our power to make sure this consignment arrives as soon as possible.

Die Verzögerung ist durch Komplikationen beim Zoll bedingt, von denen alle Lieferungen in die USA betroffen sind. Wir tun alles, was in unserer Macht steht um zu gewährleisten, dass diese Lieferung so bald wie möglich ankommt.

Since this delay is beyond our control we cannot assume any liability, but your claim has been passed on to our insurance company, who will get in touch with you in due course.

Da diese Verzögerung nicht durch uns verschuldet wurde, können wir keine Haftung übernehmen. Ihre Ansprüche wurden jedoch an unsere Versicherung weitergeleitet, die sich zu gegebener Zeit mit Ihnen in Verbindung setzen wird.

Fehler einräumen

We very much regret having given you cause for complaint. The discrepancy in our invoice was due to a clerical error. It has now been rectified and we enclose our modified invoice / a credit note.

Es tut uns sehr leid, Ihnen Anlass zur Beschwerde gegeben zu haben. Die Ungereimtheiten in unserer Rechnung waren Folge eines Bearbeitungsfehlers. Wir haben dies berichtigt und fügen die geänderte Rechnung / eine Gutschrift bei.

We have investigated the cause of the problem and have found that a mistake was made because of an

Wir sind der Ursache des Problems nachgegangen und mussten feststellen, dass der Irrtum aufgrund eines Buchungs-

accounting error / a typing error. This has now been corrected.

fehlers / eines Tippfehlers entstanden war. Dieser wurde mittlerweile korrigiert.

Maßnahmen ankündigen

We were sorry to learn of the unsatisfactory service you experienced from our maintenance engineer. Your annoyance is quite understandable. We have started enquiries to discover the cause of the problem.

Es tat uns leid zu erfahren, dass Sie mit dem Service unseres Wartungsingenieurs nicht zufrieden waren, und Ihr Ärger ist sehr verständlich. Wir haben Nachforschungen eingeleitet um die Ursache des Problems herauszufinden.

If you are prepared to keep the damaged goods, we will invoice them at a reduced rate / at 50% of the list price.

Wenn Sie bereit sind, die beschädigte Ware zu behalten, werden wir sie Ihnen zu einem reduzierten Preis / mit einer Ermäßigung von 50% des Listenpreises berechnen.

We have taken the matter up with the forwarding agents and will inform you of the results.

Wir sind dabei die Angelegenheit mit dem Spediteur zu besprechen und werden Sie vom Ergebnis in Kenntnis setzen.

We have now taken steps to ensure that such a misunderstanding does not occur in future.

Wir haben mittlerweile Schritte unternommen, um sicherzustellen, dass ein derartiges Missverständnis in Zukunft nicht mehr vorkommt.

 ANMERKUNGEN

→ Einige besonders wichtige Wörter:
to be concerned: besorgt / betroffen sein
the consignment: der Auftrag / die Lieferung
the delay: die Verzögerung
the carrier: der Spediteur
the premises: die Geschäftsräume, das Anwesen
to apologize: sich entschuldigen
a clerical error: ein Bearbeitungsfehler
the liability: die Haftung

→ Beachten Sie die Redewendung **on arrival**, die dem deutschen „bei Erhalt / Ankunft" entspricht.

→ Für das Verb „abschicken / erledigen" gibt es im Englischen zwei Schreibweisen: **to dispatch** oder **to despatch**.

⏰ SIE SIND DRAN!

• We were _____ to learn _____ your letter _____ 5th June that the _____ of porcelain plates was damaged on arrival. We have arranged _____ a replacement to be _____ immediately.

• We have _____ that a mistake was _____ in our dispatch _____ . We _____ for the inconvenience this has _____ you, and will be _____ the missing goods as soon as possible.

• Please accept our sincere _____ for the delay, which is due _____ a recent spate of strikes in this country. We are _____ _____ in our power to _____ this consignment _____ as soon as possible.

• We _____ having given you cause _____ . The discrepancy was _____ a typing error, which has now been _____ . We enclose a _____ invoice.

⊶—┴ Lösung auf Seite 145

21 STELLENANGEBOTE UND BEWERBUNGEN

Aufgrund der vielen zusätzlichen Aufträge, die infolge der Messe eingingen, und weil Luxiphon jetzt offizieller Hoflieferant der englischen Königin ist, braucht Herr Müller eine Assistentin oder einen Assistenten. Er beschließt eine Anzeige in die „Times" zu setzen und erhält interessante Antwortschreiben …

A German manufacturer of luxury telephones with important business connections in Great Britain invites applications for the post of

ASSISTANT
TO THE EXPORT MANAGER

Candidates should speak fluent German and have at least two years' experience in international business and / or in business training. Starting salary will be in the range £17–20,000 pa depending on age and experience. Please send applications to:

Mr J Müller Export Manager Luxiphon
Magdeburger Str. 250 10785 Berlin GERMANY

Janet Martin
12 Harcourt Road
LONDON SW1.

Mr J Müller   18th November 19…
Export Manager
Luxiphon
Magdeburger Str. 250
10785 Berlin

Dear Mr Müller

I should like (1) _____ assistant to the Export Manager,
(2) _____ in *The Times* of November 1st.
(3) _____ business school in 1989, where I specialised in
international business, I began working for the marketing department of United
Telecom. It was there that I came across your products for which I have
always had a high regard. I should be delighted to have the opportunity to
work for your company, in order to (4) _____ in the field of
telecommunications in a challenging international environment.
(5) _____ which will give you further particulars of my
career (6) _____. I am (7) _____ at any time,
and should be happy to come to Berlin if necessary.

I look forward to (8) _____ .

Yours sincerely

Janet Martin

Janet Martin

Brief 28: Lösung auf Seite 138

Vervollständigen Sie das Bewerbungsschreiben:

(1) *Sich für eine Stelle bewerben:*
to be the
to be considered for the post of
to propose myself as

(2) *Sich auf eine Zeitungsannonce beziehen:*
as seen
as appeared
as advertised

(3) *Die Ausbildung ansprechen:*
Having graduated from
Having got through
Having finished with

(4) *„meine Kenntnisse erweitern":*
enlarge my experiment
broaden my experience
widen my knowledge

(5) *„Beiliegend finden Sie meinen*
Lebenslauf":
I include my curriculum vitae
My curriculum vitae is enclosed
Enclosed is my curriculum vitae

(6) *„bis zum heutigen Tag":*
to date
until now
until here

(7) *Für ein Gespräch zur Verfügung*
stehen:
keen on being interviewed
waiting for my interview
available for interview

(8) *Eine Antwort erwarten:*
your acceptance
a positive reply
hearing from you

 REDEWENDUNGEN

Sich auf eine Annonce beziehen

I see from your advertisement in the
... (newspaper) that you have a
vacancy for a... .
It was with great interest that I read
the advertisement for... .
I was interested to learn that your
company is currently recruiting /
wishes to recruit... .

Aus Ihrer Anzeige in ... (Zeitung) ersehe
ich, dass Sie eine Stelle für ...
anzubieten haben.
Mit großem Interesse habe ich die
Stellenanzeige für ... gelesen.
Mit Interesse habe ich erfahren, dass Ihre
Firma zur Zeit ... einstellt / einstellen
möchte.

Sich für eine Stelle bewerben

I should like / I wish to apply for the
post of... .

Ich möchte mich für die Stelle als ...
bewerben.

Unaufgeforderte Bewerbung

I would be interested to learn / know
whether you have a vacancy for... .

I am writing to inquire about the
possibility of working for your
company.
I am looking for a post in... .

Ich bin an einer Tätigkeit als ... interes-
siert und wüsste gern, ob Sie eine
entsprechende Stelle anzubieten haben.
Hiermit möchte ich mich nach der
Möglichkeit einer Mitarbeit in Ihrer
Firma erkundigen.
Ich suche eine Stelle auf dem Gebiet /
im Bereich ... .

Informationen über die Stelle anfordern

Please send me further details of the post.

I would be obliged if you could forward a copy of the application form to me at the above address.

Bitte informieren Sie mich ausführlicher über den betreffenden Posten.

Ich wäre Ihnen dankbar, wenn Sie mir eine Kopie des Bewerbungsbogens an obige Adresse schicken könnten.

Über sich und seine berufliche Erfahrung sprechen

For the past... years I have been employed as a... .

I was responsible for... .

I was in charge of... .

I specialise in... .

This is a post for which I believe I am ideally suited.

I gained wide experience in market research in the marketing department at Peters & Sons Ltd.

·I have already acquired some experience in... .

I speak fluent English and French.

I feel I have the necessary training and qualities needed for the post of... .

I am eager to undertake new responsibilities in a challenging post.

I am keen to broaden my knowledge in the field of... .

Während der letzten ... Jahre war ich als ... angestellt.

Ich war für ... verantwortlich.

Ich hatte die Aufsicht über ... .

Mein Spezialgebiet ist ... .

Ich glaube für diese Stelle besonders geeignet zu sein.

Ich konnte bei Peters & Sons vielfältige Erfahrungen in den Bereichen Marktforschung und Marketing sammeln.

Ich habe schon allerhand Erfahrungen im Bereich / in ... gesammelt.

Ich spreche fließend Englisch und Französisch.

Ich bin überzeugt, dass ich die erforderliche Ausbildung und die nötigen Eigenschaften für diese Stelle als ... mitbringe.

Ich möchte sehr gern neue Verantwortung in einer anspruchsvollen Stellung übernehmen.

Ich bin sehr daran interessiert, meine Kenntnisse auf dem Gebiet / im Bereich von ... zu vertiefen.

Auf seinen Lebenslauf verweisen

I enclose / attach a copy of my curriculum vitae which will give you further particulars / more complete details of my career to date.

In der Anlage finden Sie meinen Lebenslauf mit weiteren Einzelheiten / vollständigen Angaben zu meiner beruflichen Laufbahn.

Schlussformulierungen

I will be happy to supply any other details you may require.

I would greatly appreciate the opportunity of an interview.

Zur Beantwortung weiterer Fragen stehe ich Ihnen gern zur Verfügung.

Ich würde mich sehr freuen, die Gelegenheit zu einem Gespräch mit Ihnen zu erhalten.

I can make myself available for interview at any time.	*Für einen Gesprächstermin kann ich mich jederzeit freimachen.*
I am available for interview at your convenience.	*Wann immer es Ihnen recht ist, stehe ich für einen Gesprächstermin zur Verfügung.*
I can only come to an interview on Fridays.	*Gesprächstermine kann ich leider nur für freitags vereinbaren.*
I shall be available from 12th May onwards.	*Ab 12. Mai bin ich verfügbar.*
The names of two referees are given below.	*Die Namen zweier Personen, die mir gern Referenzen ausstellen werden, finden Sie nachfolgend.*
I look forward to hearing from you.	*Ich freue mich auf Ihre Antwort.*
Hoping for a favourable reply.	*In der Hoffnung auf eine positive Antwort verbleibe ich … .*

 ## ANMERKUNGEN

→ Die Reihenfolge der einzelnen Schritte eines Bewerbungsschreibens sollte folgendermaßen aussehen:
- Die angestrebte Stelle nennen (mit entsprechendem Verweis: Zeitungsanzeige, Empfehlung).
- Sich vorstellen (Ausbildung, Erfahrungen auf verschiedenen Gebieten ansprechen).
- Die eigenen Beweggründe für diese Bewerbung darlegen.
- Auf den Lebenslauf, die Möglichkeit eines Gesprächs und eventuelle Referenzen verweisen.
- Abschließend die Hoffnung auf eine positive Antwort zum Ausdruck bringen.

SIE SIND DRAN!

- I wish _____ the post of salesman as advertised _____ Tuesday's *Herald Tribune*. This is a _____ for which I believe I am _____ suited.

- I _____ for a post _____ computer programming _____ a large international company. For the _____ 5 years I _____ employed _____ computer programmer _____ Hi-Tech Inc. I speak _____ Spanish and have _____ experience of working abroad.

Lösung auf Seite 145

- *Antworten Sie auf folgende Annonce:*

A large international cosmetics company based in London invites applications for the post of MARKETING MANAGER. Candidates should have over five years' work experience in the field of marketing, and have a good working knowledge of at least two foreign languages. Starting salary will be in the range £25-30,000 pa, to be negotiated. Please send applications and a detailed CV to:

The Personnel Manager Harriett Cosmetics Company Ltd 25 King's Road London SW1 England

---

Lösung auf Seite 146

22 LEBENSLAUF

Einige Anmerkungen vorab:

→ Zur Rubrik **education** (Schulbildung):
A-level entspricht der deutschen Abiturprüfung, **3 A-levels** bedeutet, dass man in drei bestimmten Fächern diese Prüfung abgelegt hat.
Standards in Hochschulen sind in unterschiedlichen Ländern nicht immer einfach zu vergleichen.
BA (Bachelor of Arts), BSc (Bachelor of Science) sind Hochschulabschlüsse, die etwa dem Vordiplom bzw. der Zwischenprüfung nach 4 Semestern entsprechen.
MA (Master of Arts), MSc (Master of Science) sind Magister-Abschlüsse und erfordern zu den „Bachelors Degrees" zusätzliche Studienzeit / Prüfungen.
MBA (Master of Business Administration) entspricht etwa einem Diplom der Wirtschaftswissenschaften.

→ Beachten Sie die Formulierungen zur Beurteilung von Sprachkenntnissen. **Good working knowledge** bedeutet: gute Grundkenntnisse, ausreichend für Geschäftsverhandlungen.

→ In Großbritannien wird die Berufserfahrung chronologisch aufgeführt (die erste Stelle erscheint zuerst), während man in den USA die jetzige, bzw. letzte Arbeitsstelle zuerst nennt.

→ In einem Lebenslauf für eine Bewerbung sollte eine sehr knapp gefasste Rubrik **hobbies** nicht fehlen. Es ist auch gang und gäbe, eine Rubrik „Sonderprojekte" oder „Sonderaufträge" anzufügen: **major projects** oder **major assignments**.

→ Die Rubrik **further qualifications** kann zusätzliche Qualifikationen erwähnen (Sprach-, Informatikkurse, Führerschein usw.) sowie Zertifikate oder Diplome, die nicht von Schule oder Universität stammen, wie auch Angaben zu Personen, die Ihnen eine Empfehlung ausstellen können.

→ Falls Sie auch ein Foto beifügen, können Sie dieses, wie bei einer Bewerbung in Deutschland, oben rechts auf Ihrem Lebenslauf anheften.

CURRICULUM VITAE

NAME: Janet Martin

ADDRESS: 12 Harcourt Road London SW1 England

TEL: (0171) 5436789

DATE OF BIRTH: 27th March 1968

MARITAL STATUS: Single

NATIONALITY: British

EDUCATION:

1984-86:	Greenfields School – Yorkshire (3 A-levels)
1986-89:	Capital Business School, London MBA, specialised in International Business

LANGUAGES:

English – mother tongue
German – fluent
French – spoken
Italian – good working knowledge

PROFESSIONAL EXPERIENCE:

Summer 1987:	Crane Engineering – Assistant to the Personnel Manager, responsible for a study on work methods
1989-1999:	United Telecom – Assistant to the Marketing Manager

HOBBIES:

Sailing – Horse riding – Jazz

FURTHER QUALIFICATIONS:

Driving licence
Good computer skills

23 BEWERBUNGEN BEANTWORTEN

ZUSAGE FÜR EIN VORSTELLUNGSGESPRÄCH

Herr Müller möchte Frau Martin sofort mitteilen, dass ihre Bewerbung in die engere Wahl gezogen wurde.

---

(1) _____

Thank you for (2) _____ the post of assistant to the Export Manager. Your curriculum vitae indicates that you may well have the qualities and experience (3) _____ .
I would be grateful if you would come to our office in Berlin for an interview on December 4th at 10 am. You (4) _____ to remain in Berlin (5) _____ as the interview procedure includes a visit to the company premises and factory. You (6) _____ for all reasonable (7) _____
I look forward to your rapid confirmation.

(8) _____

Jens Müller

Jens Müller
Export Manager

⚷ Brief 29: Lösung auf Seite 139

(1) *Die Anrede:*
    Dear Janet
    Dear Madam
    Dear Miss Martin

(2) *Welche Präposition passt hier?*
    your application to
    your application of
    your application for

(3) *Und welche ist hier richtig?*
    we are looking at
    we are looking for
    we are looking in

(4) *Welche Zeitform ist richtig?*
    will be expected
    have been expected
    must have expected

(5) „den ganzen Tag":
   during the day
   throughout the day
   since the day

(6) Eine Kostenerstattung anbieten:
   will be reimbursed
   will be refunded
   will be paid

(7) Hotel- und Reisekosten:
   hotel and travelling expenses
   hotel and voyage expenditure
   costs of lodging and travelling

(8) Die Grußformel:
   Yours faithfully
   Regards
   Yours sincerely

 REDEWENDUNGEN

Den Erhalt einer Bewerbung bestätigen

Thank you for your application for
  the post of… .

*Vielen Dank für Ihre Bewerbung, für die
  Stelle als … .*

Eine Bewerbung annehmen

We are pleased to inform you that… /
  We have pleasure in informing
  you that…
your application for the post of…
  has been successful.
you have been accepted (for the
  post of…) .
your application has been
  retained.

*Wir freuen uns Ihnen mitzuteilen /
  mitteilen zu können, dass …*
*Sie sich erfolgreich für die Stelle als …
  beworben haben.*
*wir uns (bezügl. Ihrer Bewerbung als …)
  für Sie entschieden haben.*
*Ihre Bewerbung in die engere Wahl
  gezogen wurde.*

Eine Bewerbung ablehnen

We regret to inform you that your
  application has not been accepted.

We are sorry to have to inform you
  that your name has not been
  included among those to be
  short-listed for an interview.
I am sorry to inform you that the
  post has already been filled.
We are sorry but we have no vacancies at the present time.

*Wir müssen Ihnen leider mitteilen, dass
  Ihre Bewerbung nicht angenommen
  wurde.*
*Wir bedauern, Ihnen mitteilen zu
  müssen, dass Sie nicht in die engere
  Wahl gezogen wurden.*

*Ich muss Ihnen leider mitteilen, dass die
  Stelle schon vergeben ist.*
*Wir haben leider momentan keine Stelle
  frei.*

Einen Gesprächstermin vorschlagen

We should be grateful if you would come for an interview with Mr Müller on Tuesday 9th April at 10 o'clock.	Wir wären Ihnen dankbar, wenn Sie am Dienstag, dem 9. April, um 10 Uhr zu einem Gespräch mit Herrn Müller kommen könnten.

ANMERKUNGEN

→ Beachten Sie, dass „suchen nach" im Englischen **to look FOR** heißt.

→ Wenn von „den Bewerbern" allgemein gesprochen wird, lässt man im Englischen den Artikel weg, so z. B. auch auf Seite 119 in dem Stellenangebot: **Candidates should speak...**

 SIE SIND DRAN!

- We regret _____ that we have no vacancies at _____ time.

- The _____ were all of a very high standard, and I am sorry to _____ to inform you that the post has _____ been _____ .

- Reagieren Sie mit einer positiven Antwort auf die Bewerbung eines Handelsvertreters. Schlagen Sie für Mittwoch, den 17. November, um 14 Uhr ein Gespräch vor.

Lösung auf Seite 146

24 ELEKTRONISCHE KORRESPONDENZ

Herr Müller bittet Jane Smith eine Übersetzung vom Deutschen ins Englische anzufertigen. Die Übersetzung beinhaltet Informationen zu einer Sportveranstaltung, die auch im Internet übertragen wird. Da er schon eine deutsche Datei erstellt hat und die Formate beibehalten möchte, schickt er ihr eine E-Mail mit einer angehängten Datei, damit sie die Formate übernehmen kann. Außerdem hat er eine Frage zu unterschiedlichen Anbietern und möchte die E-Mail-Adresse von Janes Bruder in Frankreich.

Subject: Translation
  Date: 1 December 1998
  From: j.müller@t-online.de
    To: JaneSmith@aol.com

Hi Jane

(1)_____ this morning. As threatened,
I have (2) _____that I would like you to translate
into English. I am assuming you have experience of this kind
of work and know about the correct tonality for the
(3) _____. Please remember to (4) _____
I have already assigned the document.

Before you do that could you please get in touch with me and
send me an estimate of how long you would need to complete
the translation and what it would cost?

By the way, I have been thinking about (5) _____. Do you
find it easy to use AOL? How do you find it in comparison to
t-online?

Could you also send me John's (6) _____?
Hoping to hear from you soon!

Regards
Jens

Brief 30: Lösung auf Seite 139

Helfen Sie nun Herrn Müller seine Mail zu vervollständigen, indem Sie jeweils einen der folgenden Begriffe auswählen.

(1) „Bezug auf Telefonat"
I enjoyed talking to
you on the phone
I talk about our
telephone conversation
As on the phone

(2) „eine Datei angehängt"
attached a file
enclosed a file
given a file

(3) Sie beziehen sich auf die Benutzer-
    gruppe
specific user group
our user group
users

(4) „die Formate beibehalten"
stick to the formats
use the formats
keep the formats

(5) Internetanbieter
providers
suppliers
deliverers

(6) E-Mail-Adresse
e-mail address
address
e-mail number

Jane Smith fragt ihr Postfach ab und bekommt nicht nur die E-Mail von Jens Müller sondern auch eine von Lars, ihrem Kollegen in Hamburg. Lars hat auch einen Text, den er gerne übersetzt hätte. Bei der Übersetzung handelt es sich um einen Brief, in dem die neue europäische Währung als Hauswährung vorgeschlagen wird.

Subject: Translation
Date: 1 December 1998
From: l.fricke@t-online.de
To: JaneSmith@aol.com

Hi Jane

(1)_____ but I have a translation I desperately need doing by this afternoon. Can you (2)_____ at some point? (3) _____ the Euro.

Before you start, could you please (4)_____ and send me an estimate of how long you'll need and what it would cost? Hoping to hear from you soon!

(5)_____!
Lars

⊶———🔑 Brief 31: Lösung auf Seite 139

Helfen Sie nun Lars seine Mail zu vervollständigen, indem Sie jeweils einen der folgenden Begriffe auswählen.

(1) „entschuldige' die Störung"
Sorry to disturb you
I hope I am not inconveniencing you
As I mentioned on the phone this morning

(2) „sie 'reinschieben"
fit it in
complete it
translate it

(3) „Bei dem Text handelt es sich um"
It's about
The text is about
It's talking about

(4) „Dich mit mir in Verbindung setzen"
get in touch with me
write to me
mail me

(5) „Paß auf Dich auf!"
Take care!
Be careful!
See you soon!

 REDEWENDUNGEN

attachment	angehängte Datei
browser	Browser
create your own web site	eine Internetseite erstellen
dial in	sich einwählen
download	herunterladen
electronic correspondence	elektronische Korrespondenz
e-mail address	E-Mail-Adresse
favo(u)rites	Favoriten
forward a mail	eine Nachricht / Mail weiterleiten
gateway	Gateway
import files in another / the same format	Dateien in einem anderen Format / in demselben Format importieren
Internet access	Internet Zugang
Internet user	Internetbenutzer / in
mailbox	elektronisches Postfach
provider	Anbieter
receive a mail	eine Nachricht / Mail empfangen
recipient	Empfänger
send a mail	eine Nachricht / Mail senden
shareware	Shareware
store / file	ablegen

subscribe	abonnieren
surf the Internet	im Internet rumstöbern
unsubscribe	Abo kündigen
web site	Webseite
zipped file	komprimierte (gezippte) Datei
If you need any further information, do not hesitate to contact us by e-mail.	Falls Sie weitere Informationen wünschen, zögern Sie nicht uns per E-Mail zu kontaktieren / mit uns per E-Mail in Verbindung zu setzen.
Why not visit our web site?	Besuchen Sie unsere Webseite!

 ANMERKUNGEN

→ Denken Sie daran, dass E-Mails im Englischen oft sehr locker formuliert werden!
→ Sie werden oft feststellen, dass die Groß- und Kleinschreibung in den E-Mails nicht so ernst genommen wird.
→ Abkürzungen werden sehr oft gebraucht, z. B. **tifn = that's it for now** - das wäre es im Moment; **TIA = thanks in advance** - danke im voraus; **BTW = by the way** - übrigens; **FAQ = frequently asked questions** - häufig gestellte Fragen, u.s.w.
→ **Snail mail** (üblicher Postweg) ist das sogenannte „Gegenteil" von E-Mail.

 SIE SIND DRAN!

If you would like more information about our company, why not (1) _____ ?

Kevin often (2) _____ the Internet to keep up with what is going on in the automotive sector.

Manuela received a really funny e-mail from Thomas and wanted to show it to her colleague in Munich so she (3) _____ the mail.

It is always a good idea to compare the fees different (4) _____ charge for Internet access before getting yourself an e-mail account.

⌐━━⌐ Lösung auf Seite 146

MUSTERBRIEFE UND LÖSUNGEN

BE = Britisches Englisch AE = Amerikanisches Englisch

ANREDE UND GRUSSFORMEL *(VGL. SEITE 13)*

Anrede:	Grußformel BE:	Grußformel AE:
Dear Sir / Madam	Yours faithfully	Yours truly
Dear Mr Shaw *(Geschäftspartner – formell)*	Yours sincerely	Yours truly Sincerely
Dear Sarah *(eine Freundin)*	Best wishes Yours	All the best Best wishes Regards
Dear David *(Geschäftspartner – informell)*	Best wishes Regards	Sincerely
Dear Mrs Wilks *(Geschäftspartnerin – informell)*	Best wishes Regards	Sincerely
To whom it may concern	–	Yours truly

1 RESERVIERUNGEN VORNEHMEN

Brief 1

(1) Dear Sir / Madam,

(2) I would like (3) to book a single room at your hotel *(4) for the week* of 19th-26th February. *(5) I require* a room with a view of the gardens, a telephone, and a private bathroom with shower.

(6) I should be grateful if you would confirm my booking *(7) as soon as possible*, and if you could *(8) give me an indication of* your rates per night including breakfast.

(9) Should you have no vacancies, please could you give me the address of a suitable hotel in the Birmingham area?

(10) Yours faithfully,

2 TERMINE VEREINBAREN

Brief 2 (geschäftlich)

(1) Dear Mrs Johnson

(2) As mentioned in my letter of January 12th, *(3) I am planning to be* in Birmingham next week for the International Telecommunications Fair. *(4) You may be interested to know* that *(5) we have recently* brought out a number of new models, and I would have great pleasure in demonstrating them to you at some point during the week. *(6) May I suggest* Tuesday 18th at 4 o'clock at your office?

(7) Should this not be convenient, you might like to propose an alternative arrangement. *(8) Would you kindly confirm* this appointment as soon as possible?

Should you have any further queries regarding our products, *(9) please do not hesitate to contact me.* I look forward to our next meeting.

Yours sincerely

Brief 3 (privat)

(1) Dear George

(2) I am due to be in Birmingham next week *(3) on business*, and I was wondering if *(4) we could meet* somewhere for dinner; it seems such a long time since we last saw each other. *(5) How about* the White Horse Inn *(6) on Tuesday* at 8?

Let me know during the week whether *(7) this suits you.* If you cannot make it maybe we can *(8) come to some other arrangement.*

(9) Looking forward to seeing you again!

(10) With best wishes

3 RESERVIERUNGEN BESTÄTIGEN

Brief 4 (positiv)

(1) Dear Mr Müller

(2) Thank you for your letter of 4th February *(3) requesting us to book* a single room with bath and shower and a view of the gardens.
(4) I have reserved the accommodation you describe *(5) for the period* you require, and *(6) should be grateful* if you would *(7) forward a deposit* of £20 as soon as possible *(8) to confirm* the reservation.
We *(9) look forward to* your stay with us.
Yours sincerely

Brief 5 (negativ)

Dear Mr Müller

Thank you for your letter of 4th February requesting us to book a single room with bath and shower and a view of the gardens.
Unfortunately *(1) we are fully booked* for the period you require because of the International Telecommunications Fair. However, *(2) we are able to recommend* an alternative hotel, also a member of the Palace chain of hotels. Although *(3) it has the slight inconvenience* of being located on the outskirts of the city, *(4) I am confident* you will find the hotel *(5) to your total satisfaction* and its surroundings most pleasant.
The address is: [......]
We remain *(6) at your service* for any future reservations you might wish to make.

Yours sincerely

4 TERMINE BESTÄTIGEN

Brief 6 (annehmen – geschäftlich)

(1) Dear Mr Müller

(2) Thank you for your letter of 10th February. *(3) I would like to confirm* that I *(4) will be available* to see you *(5) at my office* on Tuesday 18th *(6) at the time you propose.*

(7) Yours sincerely

Brief 7 (verschieben – geschäftlich)

Dear Mr Müller

With reference to your letter of 10th February, *(1) I regret* to inform you that *(2) I shall not be available* to meet you on Tuesday 18th February *(3) owing to* a company meeting. However, *(4) may I suggest* we *(5) postpone the appointment* to the following day *(6) at the same time?*

I look forward to *(7) receiving an early confirmation.*

Yours sincerely

5 INFORMATIONEN EINHOLEN

Brief 8 (Auskünfte)

(1) Dear Sir

(2) Having recently visited your stand at the International Telecommunications Fair in Birmingham, *(3) I was interested to see* that you produce some very innovative designs of luxury telephones.
(4) We are importers of quality electrical and office machinery, and feel *(5) there is a promising market* here for your type of product. *(6) Could you*

please send further details of your '20s style and pyramidal models, *(7) as well as (8) a copy* of your current catalogue showing prices and colour ranges if possible?
(9) We look forward to an early reply.

Yours faithfully

Brief 9 (Sonderwünsche)

Dear Sir

(1) While recently visiting your stand at the International Telecommunications Fair in Birmingham, *(2) I was very impressed with* your company's original designs and variety of models.
(3) I would be interested to know whether you produce a gold-coloured version of model number 36.
(4) Furthermore, (5) I wanted to enquire whether it would be possible for your company to manufacture them with several small diamonds inlaid in the receiver.
(6) Should you be able to satisfy these requirements, please inform my secretary at the above address as soon as possible, so that we can proceed with the appropriate arrangements.

Yours faithfully

6 BESTELLUNGEN AUFGEBEN

Brief 10

(1) Dear Mr Müller

(2) Thank you for your quotation of March 1st. We have pleasure in *(3) placing an order* with you for the following :

QUANTITY	NAME	MODEL	COLOUR	PRICE
50	Mars	M. 234	Green	£25.56
25	Princess	P.52	Pink	£30.05
70	Duo	D.07	Turquoise	£22.90

(4) Please acknowledge this order by returning the duplicate to us, *(5) duly signed.*

(6) Yours sincerely

7 BESTELLUNGEN BEANTWORTEN

Brief 11

(1) Dear Mr Cunningham

Thank you for *(2) your order no. 67* dated 6th March. *(3) As requested, (4) we enclose* the duplicate *(5) duly signed* in acknowledgement of your order. Our dispatch department *(6) is currently processing* your order and will inform you when *(7) the consignment* is *(8) ready for delivery.*

(9) We thank you for your custom and *(10) look forward to* being of service to you again in the near future.

Yours sincerely

8 KOSTENVORANSCHLÄGE

Brief 12

Dear Mr Stewart

(1) In reply to your letter of 9th April, *(2) we have pleasure in enclosing* a detailed quotation for the models of telephones specified. Besides those models that were on display at the International Telecommunications Fair, *(3) we have a wide range of* other de-

signs, as illustrated in our catalogue, also enclosed.

All our equipment is *(4) of a high standard* and comes with a five year guarantee. A number of accessories *(5) are available* with some of the models. Installation *(6) is carried out free of charge* by any one of our two thousand service centres located throughout Europe.
Furthermore, we are able to offer a 5% discount *(7) for any orders exceeding* £2,000.

All models can be supplied, *(8) subject to availability*, 3 months from the date on which we receive your firm order. Our cif prices are for sea / land transport only; if you require the goods to be sent by air freight, this will be charged at extra cost.

We look forward to receiving your order.

Yours sincerely

9 ZAHLUNGS-BEDINGUNGEN

Brief 13

(1) Dear Mrs Donovan

(2) We refer to your *(3) recent inquiry* regarding our *(4) conditions of payment. (5) Our terms are* 30 days net, but we can allow you *(6) two months' credit* for *(7) subsequent orders.*
Payment *(8) should be made* by irrevocable letter of credit or order cheque.

(9) We look forward to receiving your initial order.

(10) Yours sincerely

10 LIEFERBEDINGUNGEN

Brief 14

Dear Ms Webster

(1) We refer to your order no. 33. *(2) Delivery will be made* within two months of *(3) receipt of your order. (4) As arranged*, the consignment will be transported *(5) by rail and sea freight* fob from Birmingham to your warehouse in Atlanta, Georgia.

Our prices are cif for sea / land transport to Georgia. *(6) If you require* more rapid delivery, *(7) we can arrange* for the goods to be sent by air freight, but *(8) this will be charged at extra cost*. Insurance is *(9) payable by you*.

(10) We thank you for your custom, and will be pleased to answer any further queries you might have regarding the shipment.

Yours truly *(AE)*

11 ZAHLUNGS-ERINNERUNGEN

Brief 15

(1) Dear Mr Hughes

We would like to *(2) draw your attention to* our invoice No. 254 dated September 5th. *(3) As we have not yet received* payment, *(4) we should be grateful* if you would *(5) forward your remittance* as soon as possible. *(6) If you have already sent* the amount due, please *(7) ignore this reminder*.

(8) Yours truly (AE)

12 VERHANDLUNGEN UND VEREINBARUNGEN

Brief 16

Dear Sir or Madam

We are manufacturers of telephone answering machines and *(1) are seeking* a European manufacturer of compatible products with a view to entering into a commercial partnership. We would like to offer our services as commercial agents for your products in the United States, *(2) in exchange for* your representation of our products on the European market. Please find enclosed a brochure describing our company.

As we are sure *(3) you are aware*, the US market offers excellent potential for your type of product, and *(4) we feel confident* that you will appreciate how much *(5) your company could benefit* from such a partnership. As for ourselves, we have reason to believe that the market *(6) is opening up* in Europe for our products and consider that the best way *(7) to take advantage of this opportunity* is to achieve a commercial presence via a European company.

We hope you will *(8) give this proposal your kind consideration*, and look forward to your reply.

Yours truly *(AE)*

13 VERTRÄGE AUFSETZEN

Brief 17

Dear Mr Southampton

Agency Agreement

(1) With reference to our telephone conversation of Thursday, I am pleased to confirm the agency agreement giving you *(2) sole agency* for our products in the United States.

(3) Enclosed are two copies of our terms for the agency agreement. Would you please *(4) sign both copies* and return them to me, *(5) together with* any comments or amendments you would like to make regarding the contents? *(6) Should you have any further queries* concerning the conditions of the agency agreement *(7) please do not hesitate to contact me.*

I look forward to *(8) our forthcoming meeting* to discuss the final contract, and hope this is the beginning of a long and mutually beneficial association.

Yours truly *(AE)*

14 DANKSCHREIBEN

Brief 18 (formell)

(1) Dear Mrs Johnson

(2) I should like to thank you for *(3) the fruitful meeting* we had last Tuesday and for *(4) your kind hospitality.* It was *(5) most interesting* to visit your company and become better acquainted with your business operations.
I trust *(6) we shall shortly be receiving* your order for the new products *(7) we discussed during our meeting,* and look forward to *(8) renewed transactions* between our two companies.

(9) Yours sincerely

15 ANGEBOTE UND EINLADUNGEN

Brief 19 (formell)

(1) Dear Sir

The administrators of Buckingham Palace *(2) have pleasure in inviting you* to tender *(3) for a contract as official supplier* to Her Majesty the Queen.

(4) Please find enclosed an invitation *(5) to attend a reception* at the Palace, at which all current and potential suppliers will be present.

We look forward to *(6) your early reply.*

(7) Yours faithfully

Brief 20 (informell)

(1) Dear Sarah

I have *(2) taken the liberty of writing to you* as *(3) I am due to be* in England again soon, for the week beginning 20th June, and *(4) was wondering if we could* spend an evening together. *(5) How would you like to go to* that new play at the Royal Theatre, followed, of course, by dinner? *(6) Let me know* which day *(7) would suit you best,* and I will ask my secretary *(8) to make the necessary reservations.*

I hope you will *(9) be able to make it* as I am very much looking forward to seeing you again.

(10) Best wishes

16 EINLADUNGEN BEANTWORTEN

Brief 21 (formell)

(1) Dear Mr Blue

(2) In reply to your letter of 1st June *(3) we have pleasure in accepting* your invitation *(4) to tender for a contract* as official supplier to Her Majesty the Queen.
(5) We look forward to receiving further *(6) instructions and documentation* regarding the tender procedure.

(7) Yours sincerely

Brief 22 (formell)

Dear Sir

Mr Müller *(8) thanks* Her Majesty's Suppliers *(9) for their kind invitation* to the reception at Buckingham Palace on Friday 20th June which *(10) he has much pleasure in accepting.*

Yours faithfully

Brief 23 (informell)

(1) Dear Jens

(2) Thanks for the invitation. *(3) I would be delighted* to go to the theatre with you. The best day for me would be Monday 23rd June.
(4) It will be a pleasure to see you again!

(5) Best wishes

17 GESCHÄFTLICHE MITTEILUNGEN

Brief 24

(1) Dear Customer

(2) We have pleasure in announcing that our company has recently been accepted as official supplier to Her Majesty the Queen.

This contract *(3) comes as a reward for* the excellent quality and service *(4) we always strive to offer* our customers. To mark the event we are offering special prices on our Mars and Princess ranges if *(5) you place your order* before 1st August. We are sending you our latest catalogue *(6) under separate cover.*

We look forward to maintaining the special relationship we have with our customers and to continuing to *(7) provide them with* the prompt service and quality products *(8) they are accustomed to.*

(9) Yours sincerely

18 PERSÖNLICHE KORRESPONDENZ

Brief 25

(1) Dear Angela

(2) I was delighted to learn that you *(3) have been appointed* Regional Manager for Europe. *(4) May I wish you every success* in your new post, for which I am sure you have just *(5) the right qualities* and experience. My colleagues *(6) join me in sending you* our warmest congratulations, and we

look forward to *(7) continuing our long association.*

(8) With best wishes

19 PROBLEME UND REKLAMATIONEN

Brief 26

Dear Mr Müller

(1) We took delivery this morning of our order no. 671B.
(2) Regrettably, some of the crates were damaged, and on unpacking them we found a number of breakages. We would suggest this is due either to *(3) inadequate packing* or to an accident in transit.
As sale was on a cif basis, we presume *(4) you will be claiming compensation* from the carrier. We estimate the value of the damage at around £2,500. We will, of course, be keeping the damaged crates and their contents *(5) for inspection.*
(6) Under the terms of the guarantee, we should be most grateful if you would *(7) send a replacement* for the damaged items. A list of these is enclosed. We must ask you to *(8) attend to the matter with the utmost urgency* as this delay is *(9) causing us great inconvenience.*

We look forward to an early reply.

Yours sincerely

20 REKLAMATIONEN BEANTWORTEN

Brief 27

(1) Dear Mr Brown
We were *(2) concerned to learn from* your letter of October 3rd that the consignment of telephones ordered from us was *(3) damaged on arrival.* We *(4) very much regret the inconvenience* this has caused you.
Upon investigation, we have ascertained that the consignment was packed *(5) in the usual manner,* which *(6) in our experience* is more than adequate for a journey of the kind undertaken. Any damage *(7) occurring in transit,* however, is the responsibility of the carrier, and we have *(8) handed the matter over to* our insurance company, who will be contacting you shortly.
I have asked one of our agents to arrange to call at your *(9) premises* to inspect the damage. In the meantime, a replacement for the damaged articles was despatched today.
Once again, *(10) we apologize* for the inconvenience caused, and trust that you will find the replacements *(11) to your entire satisfaction.*

Yours sincerely

21 STELLENANGEBOTE UND BEWERBUNGEN

Brief 28

Dear Mr Müller

I should like *(1) to be considered for the post of* assistant to the Export Manager, *(2) as advertised* in "The Times" of November 1st.

(3) Having graduated from business school in 1989, where I specialised in international business, I began working for the marketing department of United Telecom. It was there that I came across your products for which I have always had a high regard. I should be delighted to have the opportunity to work for your company, in order to *(4) broaden my experience* in the field of telecommunications in a challenging international environment.

(5) Enclosed is my curriculum vitae which will give you further particulars of my career *(6) to date.* I am *(7) available for interview* at any time, and should be happy to come to Berlin if necessary.

I look forward to *(8) hearing from you.*

Yours sincerely

23 BEWERBUNGEN BEANTWORTEN

Brief 29

(1) Dear Miss Martin

Thank you for *(2) your application for* the post of assistant to the Export Manager. Your curriculum vitae indicates that you may well have the qualities and experience *(3) we are looking for.*

I would be grateful if you would come to our office in Berlin for an interview on December 4th at 10 am. You *(4) will be expected* to remain in Berlin *(5) throughout the day* as the interview procedure includes a visit to the company premises and factory. You *(6) will be reimbursed* for all reasonable *(7) hotel and travelling expenses.*

I look forward to your rapid confirmation.

(8) Yours sincerely

24 ELEKTRONISCHE KORRESPONDENZ

Brief 30

Hi Jane

(1) I enjoyed talking to you on the phone this morning. As threatened, I have *(2) attached a file* that I would like you to translate into English. I am assuming you have experience of this kind of work and know about the correct tonality for the *(3) specific user group.* Please remember to *(4) stick to the formats* I have already assigned the document.

Before you do that could you please get in touch with me and send me an estimate of how long you would need to complete the translation and what it would cost?

By the way, I have been thinking about *(5) providers.* Do you find it easy to use AOL? How do you find it in comparison to t-online?

Could you also send me John's *(6) e-mail address?*

Hoping to hear from you soon!
Regards
Jens

Brief 31

Hi Jane

(1) Sorry to disturb you but I have a translation I desperately need doing by this afternoon. Can you *(2) fit it in* at some point? *(3) It's about* the Euro.

Before you start, could you please *(4) get in touch with me* and send me an estimate of how long you'll need and what it would cost?

Hoping to hear from you soon!

(5) Take care!
Lars

SIE SIND DRAN! – LÖSUNGEN

Seite 18 / 19:

I *would like* to *rent* / hire a car *for* the month of May. I would be *grateful* if you could send me your daily *rates* for a small four-seater car, and an indication *of* the current prices of petrol in Spain.

FOR RENT

beautiful villa on the island of Jersey. Four bedrooms, each *with* private bathroom; spacious lounge which *faces* the sea; swimming pool with diving board.

Having seen your advertisement for the villa in Jersey, I *would be* interested *in booking* it from 1st-30th September. Please *confirm* at your earliest *convenience* whether this would be possible.

I would like *to rent* a caravan *for* the weekend. I *would be* grateful if you *could* send some information on the different models available, as well as an *indication* of your *current* rates.

I am *writing* to you in order to *book* a flight to Barbados *on* 10th July. I will be travelling with my wife and two children, and therefore will *require* four seats. We *would like* to travel first class. I should be *grateful* if you would confirm the booking as *soon* as possible, as I must also make arrangements to *rent* / hire a car for our stay.

Seite 26:

With reference *to* my letter *of* April 12th, I am *planning to be* in London next week. I would like to *take* the opportunity to present our new catalogue.

May I suggest 5th May *at* 3 pm? Should you be *unavailable* on this date, you might like to propose an alternative arrangement.

I *am planning* to travel to Kent *on* 15th March. The purpose of my trip *is* to visit our factory in the region. I hope to *have the* pleasure *of* meeting you during my stay. I *would* suggest 17th March *at* 5 o'clock at your office. *Please* confirm if you *are* available at this time.

I am *likely* to be in Somerset in June *for* the Flower Festival. I was *wondering* if we could meet somewhere *for* lunch. *How about* the Bull Inn on Friday *at* 2 pm?

I *hope* to be travelling to Dhaka next Monday. *I was wondering* if we could meet there *in* the evening. I would *suggest* the Hilton Hotel *at* 7 pm in the lobby.

Dear William
I am planning to come / fly to London on a business trip at the beginning of March.
I was wondering if we could meet for a drink. How about in front of Victoria Station on Monday, 8th March at 9 pm?
[Ihr Name]

Seite 31:

We *regret* to inform you *that* there are no bicycles *available* for the period you require. We *suggest* you contact the Cambridge Bicycle Centre. *They may be able* to help you.

I am writing *to confirm* your reservation *for* three first class seats on Friday's flight *to* Bangkok, arriving on 30th July. Please find enclosed your tickets and our invoice.

Thank you for your letter of 7th May. We are *pleased* to confirm your reservation *for* a yacht *from* 4th June – 3rd July. Enclosed are our charges and our conditions of hire.

With reference to *our* telephone conversation of 13th April, we are pleased *to confirm* your reservation *for a* package tour to India *for* two people.

Seite 37:

I am *afraid* I won't be able to make it *to* the theatre on Friday as I have *something else* on.

With reference to your letter *of* 6th March, I *would like* to confirm that I shall be *able* to meet you *on* 20th May to discuss a possible partnership.

Much *to my regret*, I am obliged to cancel our *forthcoming* meeting, *owing to* a sudden illness. I *apologize* for any *inconvenience* caused, and I shall contact you as soon as possible to *arrange* another meeting.

In reply to your letter *of* 20th January, I should *be* pleased to meet you *on* Friday, but *would* prefer it if the meeting could be postponed to take place later in the afternoon.

Dear Thomas
I'm afraid I will have to cancel breakfast on Thursday. My boss has just told me I have to go on a business trip to Paris on Thursday and Friday.

How about breakfast next Tuesday?
Hope to see you then!
Yours
[Ihr Name]

Seite 44:

While *recently visiting* your factory, *I was* very impressed with your manufacturing procedures. *I would* be interested to know *whether* you produce smaller sizes of model number 2. I would like to *order* 500 pairs *of* sunglasses, model no. 546. *If you can* satisfy these requirements, please *inform my* secretary at the *above* address.

Having *visited* your stand *at* the trade fair, I would *be grateful for* details about your telephones, model no. 99. Please *contact* me *at* my office under this number.

We are wholesalers in the tea trade, and we *would like* some information *on* the types of tea you produce. Would you *kindly* send *us* your latest catalogue *with* prices, as well as a selection of samples?

Having read your advertisement in the local newspaper, I would be very grateful if you could send me the free catalogue you mentioned with samples.

Seite 49:

I *would like to order* two large turkeys for Christmas Day. *Please acknowledge* this order by return of post.

Thank you for your quotation *of* 6th November. We *have* pleasure *in placing* an order *with* you for the *undermentioned* items. Please *confirm* that you can supply the goods *by* the end of the month.

Thank you *for* your quotation. We feel however that your *products* do not meet our *requirements*. We shall therefore not *place* an order with you.

We have pleasure in placing *an order for* 500 Garard hi-fis and 200 Blaster portable radios for *immediate* delivery. Please sign the *duplicate* of this order and return it to us as an acknowledgement.

We enclose our order for 20 pairs of shoes, model Cinderella, size 36 (5) for immediate delivery.

Seite 53:

We *are pleased* to acknowledge your order no. 70 *of* 5th January. We *have pleasure in confirming* that delivery will *be made* by 15th January.

Thank you for your order no. 56. Delivery will be made by 19th May as requested.

Thank you for your order no. 45. As requested we *enclose* the copy, *duly* signed *in* acknowledgement. Your order is already *being processed* and will be ready for delivery *before the end of* next week.

Thank you for your order no. 95-SP8. We regret to inform you that the goods ordered are out of stock and that delivery can only be made in three weeks' time.

Seite 57:

In reply to your inquiry of 5th December, we are pleased to *enclose* a detailed quotation *for* the goods specified. We can allow a 3% discount *on* all orders *exceeding* £50. Prices are *subject to* change without *notice*.

We are pleased *to enclose* a quotation *for* the renovation of your premises. The work carried out *carries* a guarantee of one year *subject to* your prior approval of the completed renovation. We enclose our most *recent* catalogue to give you an indication of the materials available. We also *enclose* our *latest* price list.

In *reply to* your inquiry of 1st September we are pleased *to enclose* the requested quotation *for the* goods specified. This range is a special *introductory* offer, with a 5% discount *on* your initial order. If you wish to take advantage *of* this offer, please fill *in* the *enclosed* form.

With *reference* to your enquiry *of* 8th January, we have pleasure *in* enclosing a quotation *for* the goods specified. Please let *us* have your order as soon as possible, since *supplies* are limited.

Seite 62:

Our usual *terms of payment* are 60 days *net*. We can *allow* you 1 month's further *credit* for repeat *orders*. Payment *should be made* by bank transfer.

Enclosed is our invoice *amounting to* £500. Would you kindly *forward* your remittance *in settlement* of the above as soon as possible.

We *have pleasure in* enclosing our *banker's* draft *for* £200 *in* settlement of the enclosed invoice no. 334. Please *acknowledge* receipt *by* return *of* post.

We are not in a *position* to offer credit, but we can *offer / allow* a discount *on* all orders *exceeding* £300.

We *confirm* with thanks *receipt of your* banker's draft for £572, sent in payment of order no. 910. We *are looking forward* to receiving your next order.

Seite 66:

We refer to our order of 30th October. Please note that delivery should be made by 15th November by sea and rail freight, ex works, delivery duty paid.

We *refer to* your order *for* 500 pairs of green socks. The items are *in* stock and should be ready *for* despatch by next week. Delivery *will be* made *within* one month of processing the order.

Owing *to* problems *in* our manufacturing plant, we are *unable* to deliver your order no. 77. *Unless* we receive *instructions* from you *to* the contrary, we will *assume* that your order still stands.

Seite 71:

As we *have not yet* received payment *for* our invoice no. 609, we would be grateful if you would forward *your remittance* as *soon as* possible.

Despite two previous reminders your account is *still* outstanding. *Unless* payment reaches us *within* the next seven days, we shall have to take *legal proceedings.*

Thank you for your reminder for invoice no. 703B. We have already sent the amount due and therefore can only assume that there is a problem in the accounts department.

Seite 75:

We are a trading company *specialising* in the *marketing* and *sales* of construction equipment *in* the Asian market. We *would be interested in* an agency agreement for the commercialisation of your products *in* this part of the world.

We are retailers *of* video games and *are* interested in acting as agents *for* you in Western Africa. We *enclose* our brochure detailing our activities. We look *forward to receiving* your comments *on* this proposal.

We *are a* distribution company *specialising in* computers and *would* be interested in a partnership *for* the distribution of your products, to cover the whole *of* Northern Europe. If you are interested *in* this proposal, please get in *touch* with us as soon as possible.

Seite 80:

With *reference to* your letter of 9th September, I have *pleasure* in confirming the franchise agreement authorising you to set up a branch of our company in Brazil. *Enclosed* are two copies of the franchise agreement. Please *sign both* copies and *return* one to me.

The general conditions of the contract are as follows:
The contract is *limited* initially to 5 years, but may be *renewed* for a further year *based on* an annual evaluation of your company's performance.
Our representatives work *on* a commission *basis.*
Commission is *payable on* all orders.

Seite 84:

Dear Tom and Hazel
Many thanks for the lovely evening last week. I haven't enjoyed myself so much for a long time and, Hazel, we simply loved the excellent meal – but then we didn't really expect anything else!
Hope to see you again soon!
Best wishes
[Ihr Name]

Please *accept* my warmest thanks *for* your kind *hospitality* during my visit to Nairobi last week.

I *am most grateful to* you for the useful advice and the interesting documents you gave me *on the occasion of* our last meeting.

Seite 90:

The President of Europa Ltd. *requests* the *pleasure* of your company *at* a luncheon to take *place* at the York Hotel, Chelsea *on* Thursday, 5th March, *at* 1 o'clock, in *honour of* his retirement.

We are going to the theatre next week with a few friends and *would be very pleased* if you *could* come.

Mr and Mrs Simpson request the *pleasure* of your *company* at a banquet *to be* held *at* the Ritz Hotel, on Friday 21 April, *at* 6 pm.

We *are having* some friends over *for* lunch next Sunday. We would be *very pleased* if you *could* join us.

I wondered *whether* you would be interested *in* going *to* a museum next week. Let me know whether you *are / will be able to* come.

Seite 95:

Mr and Mrs Jones *thank* Mr and Mrs Cavendish *for* their *kind* invitation *to* dinner, which they are regretfully *unable* to accept *owing* to a prior engagement.

Thanks a lot for the invitation *to* dinner. I *am afraid* I won't *be able* to make it as I am going on holiday next week.

Thank *you* very much *for your kind invitation* to spend a weekend in Glasgow. We *would be* delighted to *come.*

Seite 99:

You will be *interested to know* that we have just brought out a new *range* of hi-fi equipment. To *mark* the occasion, we *are offering* a discount on all orders *exceeding* £2000. We *have sent* you our latest catalogue *under* separate cover.

We *have pleasure* in announcing the merger of *our company* with United Motors Ltd. As *a result* of this merger we *are able* to offer a much wider *range* of cars at reduced *prices.*

To mark the opening of *our new* factory *in* New Malden, we *are offering* 5% off list-price if *we receive* your order within the next month.

You *will be* interested to know that we have recently brought *out* our *brand-new* selection *of* ozone-friendly hairsprays. You *will* find this version *of* the hairspray *even more* economical and easy to use.

Seite 104:

I was *sorry* to *hear* that you have been taken ill. Please *accept* my very best wishes for *a complete and speedy* recovery.

We were deeply sorry to hear *of* Henry's tragic death. Please *pass on* our condolences *to* his wife and family.

It came to my notice recently *that* after 15 years *doing* business together, your company *has* become one of *our* oldest customers. I *should like* to take the opportunity of *thanking* you for *your* regular patronage.

I *was pleased* to learn *that* you have been appointed Sales Manager. *I* wish you *every success* in your *new* post. With *best* wishes.

Seite 110:

We *took* delivery yesterday *of* our order no. 45K. We found on *opening / examining* the crates that several items were missing. A list of the missing articles is *enclosed*. Please arrange for *replacements* of these goods to *be sent* as soon as possible.

We *regret* to inform you that our order no. 89 *has* not arrived. This *delay* is causing us great *inconvenience* as we have a very tight production *schedule*.

I am extremely *concerned* at your repeated failure to *deliver* our consignments on time. If there is no improvement I am *afraid* we shall have to take our custom elsewhere.

I *refer* to your invoice no. 789, in which we have noticed a number of *errors*. I should *be grateful if* you would look into this and *send* us a *new* invoice.

Seite 115:

We were *concerned* to learn *from* your letter *of* 5th June that the *consignment* of porcelain plates was damaged on arrival. We have arranged *for* a replacement to be *dispatched* immediately.

We have *discovered* that a mistake was *made* in our dispatch *department*. We *apologize* for the inconvenience this has *caused* you and will be *forwarding* the missing goods as soon as possible.

Please accept our sincere *apologies* for the delay, which is due *to* a recent spate of strikes in this country. We are *doing everything* in our power to *make sure* this consignment *arrives* as soon as possible.

We *very much regret* having given you cause *for complaint*. The discrepancy was *due to* a typing error, which has now been *rectified*. We enclose a *modified* invoice.

Seite 121:

I wish *to apply for* the post of salesman as advertised *in* Tuesday's Herald Tribune. This is a *post* for which I believe I am *ideally* suited.

I *am looking* for a post *in* computer programming *with* a large international company. For the *past* 5 years I *have been* employed *as a* computer programmer *at* Hi-Tech Inc. I speak *fluent* Spanish and have *already acquired some* experience of working abroad.

Kathrin Schmidt
Hauptstr. 215
70174 Stuttgart
Germany

The Personnel   24th November 19..
Manager
Harriett Cosmetics
Company Ltd.
25 King's Road
London SW1
England

Dear Sir or Madam

I was interested to learn that your company is currently looking for a marketing manager.

For the past seven years I have worked in the marketing department of a fashion company and have been employed as assistant to the marketing manager there for just over two years now. In my position as assistant, I was responsible for liaison work with our advertising agencies in England and France and so have a good working knowledge of the two languages, as well as my own (German).

As I use your products myself, and have done for a long time now, I would be delighted to have the opportunity of working for your company and am keen to broaden my knowledge in the field of marketing.

I enclose a copy of my curriculum vitae which will give you further particulars of my career to date and will be happy to supply any other details you may require.

I am available for interview at your convenience and look forward to hearing from you in the near future.

Yours faithfully

Kathrin Schmidt

Seite 126:

We regret *to inform you* that we have no vacancies at *the present* time.

The *applicants* were all of a very high standard, and I am sorry to *have* to inform you that the post has *already* been *filled.*

Thank you for your application for the post of sales representative.
We are pleased to inform you that we would like you to come for an interview on 17th November at 2 pm.

Seite 130:

If you would like more information about our company, why not *visit our web site?*

Kevin often *surfs* the Internet to keep up with what is going on in the automotive sector.

Manuela received a really funny e-mail from Thomas and wanted to show it to her colleague in Munich so she *forwarded* the mail.

It is always a good idea to compare the fees different *providers* charge for Internet access before getting yourself an e-mail account.

NÜTZLICHE REDEWENDUNGEN

BRIEFANFANG

Informieren, ankündigen

Wir freuen uns, Ihnen mitteilen zu können ... .

We have pleasure in announcing... .

Wir freuen uns, Sie davon in Kenntnis zu setzen, ...

We are pleased to inform you... .

Es wird Sie interessieren, dass ... .

You will be interested to know that... .

Bestätigen

Wir bestätigen Ihnen (hiermit) ... .

We (hereby) write to confirm... . / This is to confirm... .

Wir freuen uns, (Ihnen) zu bestätigen ... .

We are pleased to confirm... .

Mit größtem Vergnügen (würde ich) ... .

I should be delighted to... .

Wir sind von ... sehr beeindruckt.

We are very impressed by... .

Empfang bestätigen

Wir danken Ihnen für Ihren Brief vom ... .

(We) Thank you for your letter of... . / We acknowledge with thanks your letter of... .

Wir haben ... erhalten.

We have received... .

Wir bestätigen den Erhalt von ... .

We acknowledge receipt of... .

Sich auf einen vorausgegangenen Kontakt beziehen

Bezug nehmend auf unser Telefongespräch ... .

As per / Following our telephone conversation ... .

Wie in meinem Brief vom ... erwähnt ... .

As mentioned in my letter of... .

Bezug nehmend auf Ihren Brief vom ... .

With reference to your letter of... .

Wir beziehen uns auf Ihren Brief vom ... .

We refer to your letter of... / Further to your letter of... .

Auf Anlagen hinweisen

In der Anlage erhalten Sie ... .

Please find enclosed... . / We enclose... .

Anbei finden Sie ... .

Enclosed is / are... .

Wir freuen uns, ... beizufügen.

We have pleasure in enclosing... .

Wir schicken … mit getrennter Post.	*We are sending… under separate cover.*
Wir freuen uns Ihnen … vorzulegen / zu unterbreiten.	*We are pleased to submit… .*

Einem Termin zustimmen

Montag um 10 Uhr würde mir zusagen.	*Monday at 10 am would suit me perfectly.*
Dienstag passt mir sehr gut.	*Tuesday is fine by me. (informell)*

Ablehnen, ein Angebot zurückweisen

Es tut uns leid, Ihnen mitteilen zu müssen, dass … .	*We regret to have to announce / to have to inform you that… .*
Es tut uns leid, Sie davon in Kenntnis zu setzen … .	*We regret to inform you… .*
Leider fürchte ich, dass … .	*Unfortunately, I am afraid that… .*
Sehr zu meinem Bedauern … .	*Much to my regret… .*
Ich kann nur … bedauern.	*I can only regret… .*
Wir sind nicht in der Lage, … anzunehmen.	*We are not in a position to accept… .*
Es ist mir nicht möglich, … .	*It is not possible for me to… .*
Es kann keine Frage sein, dass … .	*There can be no question of… .*
Es steht außer Frage.	*It is out of the question.*

ANFRAGEN

Eine Bitte formulieren

Könnten Sie … ?	*Could you please… ?*
Ich wäre Ihnen dankbar, wenn Sie … .	*I should be grateful if you would… .*
Ich wäre Ihnen dankbar, wenn Sie … könnten.	*I would be obliged if you would… .*
Wir wären dankbar, wenn … .	*We should be glad if… .*
Wir wären (sehr) dankbar für … .	*We would be (most) grateful for… .*
Wären Sie so freundlich, … ?	*Would you kindly… ?*
Wäre es Ihnen möglich, … zu … ?	*Would it be possible for you to… ?*
Würden Sie bitte … ?	*Please would you… .*
Wir möchten … .	*We would like… .*
Sie werden gebeten, … .	*You are requested… .*

Informationen einholen

Könnten Sie uns mitteilen, ob … ?	*Could / Would you let us know if… ?*
Wir wüssten gern, ob … oder … .	*We would be interested to know whether / if… .*

Könnten Sie mir sagen, ob … ?	Could you tell me whether / if… ?
Bitte nachsenden an … .	Please forward to… .
Bitte schicken Sie mir … .	Please send me… .
Könnten Sie mir freundlicherweise … zuschicken?	Would you kindly send me… ?
Bitte machen Sie mir genauere An-gaben zu … .	Please give me details of… .

Um eine Antwort oder Bestätigung bitten

Bitte antworten Sie …	Please reply…
umgehend.	without delay.
postwendend.	by return of post.
Bitte lassen Sie (es) uns schnellst-möglich wissen.	Please let us know as soon as possible.
Schicken Sie Ihre Antwort bitte an …	Please send your reply to… .
Setzen Sie sich bitte mit … in Verbindung.	Please contact… .
Bitte bestätigen Sie … .	Would you please confirm… ?

VORSCHLÄGE, ANGEBOTE, EINLADUNGEN

Vorschlagen

Darf ich vorschlagen, … ?	May I suggest… ?
Ich würde vorschlagen, … .	I would suggest… .
Wir können Ihnen … vorschlagen.	We are able to suggest… .
Sie könnten … .	You could… .
Sie könnten vielleicht … .	You might… .
Ich schlage vor, dass … .	I propose that… .
Was meinen Sie zu … ?	What would you say about… ?
Es wäre sinnvoll, … .	It would be sensible… .

Ein Angebot machen

Wir bieten (Ihnen) … (an).	We are offering… .
Wir können Ihnen … anbieten.	We are able to offer you… .
Diese Ware ist im Sonderangebot.	These goods are / This product is on special offer.
Wir würden sehr gern … .	We would be delighted to… .
Wenn es Ihnen nichts ausmacht, … .	If you don't mind… . (informell)

Einladen

Ich möchte Sie … einladen.	I should like to invite you… .
Wir würden uns sehr freuen, wenn Sie zu / für … zu uns kämen.	We should be delighted if you would join us for… .
Ich wäre sehr erfreut … .	I should be delighted… .

REKLAMATIONEN

Reklamieren

Wir möchten Sie daran erinnern, dass … .	*We would like to remind you that… .*
Leider müssen wir Ihnen mitteilen, dass … sich nun beträchtlich verspätet hat.	*We regret to inform you that… is now considerably overdue.*
Wir bedauern, Ihnen mitteilen zu müssen, dass … noch nicht angekommen ist.	*We regret to have to inform you that… has not yet arrived.*
Bitte bringen Sie in Erfahrung, warum die Lieferung von … noch nicht erfolgt ist.	*Please look into the non-delivery of…*
Wir bitten um eine Überprüfung / Erklärung … .	*We should like to query… .*
Leider muss ich mich über … beschweren.	*I regret to have to complain about… .*

Auf ein Problem aufmerksam machen

Wir möchten Sie auf die Tatsache hinweisen, dass … .	*We would like to draw your attention to the fact that… .*
Es / Da muss ein Fehler vorliegen.	*There must be some mistake.*

GEWISSHEIT, VERMUTUNG, ZWEIFEL

Gewissheit zum Ausdruck bringen

Es ist klar, dass … .	*It is clear that… .*
Es besteht kein Zweifel, dass … .	*There is no doubt that… .*
Wir sind (davon) überzeugt, dass … .	*We are convinced / confident that… .*
Wir werden (es) nicht versäumen, zu … .	*We shall not fail to… .*

Vermutungen aufstellen

Es ist sehr wahrscheinlich, dass … .	*It is quite possible that… .*
Es hat den Anschein, dass … .	*It would seem that… .*
Alles scheint darauf hinzuweisen, dass … .	*Everything seems to point to the fact that… .*
Sollte dies unpassend / ungelegen sein, … .	*Should this not be convenient… .*
Sollten Sie nicht verfügbar sein, … .	*Should you be unavailable… .*
Sollte dies nicht mit … übereinstimmen, … .	*If this does not fit in with… . (z. B. Pläne) / If this does not correspond with… . (z. B. Rechnungen)*

Zweifel und Befürchtungen zum Ausdruck bringen

Leider … .	*Unfortunately… .*
Ich fürchte, dass … .	*I am afraid that… .*
Wir bezweifeln, dass … .	*We doubt very much whether… .*
Es könnte eine Verzögerung eintreten.	*This could cause a delay.*

SICH ENTSCHULDIGEN

Es tat uns leid zu hören, dass … .	*We were sorry to hear that… .*
Es tut uns sehr leid um … / , dass … .	*We are very sorry for / that… .*
Wir entschuldigen uns für … .	*We apologize for… .*
Wir bitten Sie ganz herzlich, uns für … zu entschuldigen.	*Please accept our sincere apologies for… .*
Wir müssen uns für … entschuldigen.	*We must apologize for… .*
Bitte entschuldigen Sie … .	*Do forgive us for… .*

GLÜCK- UND GENESUNGSWÜNSCHE, BEILEIDSERKLÄRUNGEN

Herzliche Glückwünsche.	*Many congratulations.*
Wir senden unsere herzlichsten Glückwünsche.	*Please accept our warmest congratulations.*
Wir wünschen Ihnen allen erdenklichen Erfolg.	*We wish you every success.*
Ich sende Ihnen meine (aller)besten Wünsche für eine rasche Genesung.	*I send you my (very) best wishes for a speedy recovery.*
Ich möchte Ihnen alles Gute zum Geburtstag wünschen.	*I would like to wish you a very happy birthday.*
Darf ich Ihnen mein herzliches Beileid ausdrücken?	*May I offer you my sincere condolences?*

SICH BEDANKEN

formell:

Ich möchte mich aufrichtig für … bedanken.	*I should like to express my sincere thanks for… .*
Wir sind Ihnen für die Art und Weise, in der Sie …, zu größter Dankbarkeit verpflichtet.	*We owe you our most sincere thanks for the way in which you… .*
Es war sehr freundlich von Ihnen … .	*It was most kind of you… .*

Wir möchten Ihnen für … danken.	*We should like to thank you for… .*
Wir bedanken uns sehr für … .	*We are most grateful for… .*
Wir bedanken uns ganz herzlich für … .	*Please accept our warmest thanks for… .*
Wir möchten unserer Dankbarkeit / unserem aufrichtigen Dank für … Ausdruck geben.	*We should like to express our gratitude / our sincere thanks for… .*

informell:

Wir danken für … .	*Thank you for… .*
Danke für … .	*Thank you for… .*
Vielen Dank für … .	*Many thanks for… .*

BRIEFSCHLUSS

Wir möchten uns nochmals für Ihre Hilfe bedanken.	*Thanking you once again for your help.*
Mit bestem Dank im Voraus.	*Thanking you in advance.*
Bei etwaigen Rückfragen stehen wir Ihnen gerne jederzeit zur Verfügung.	*Please do not hesitate to contact us if you require any further information.*
Wir freuen uns darauf, … zu be-kommen.	*We look forward to receiving… .*
Wir freuen uns auf eine baldige Antwort.	*We look forward to hearing from you soon.*

E-MAIL

Falls Sie weitere Informationen brauchen, zögern Sie nicht uns per E-Mail zu kontaktieren / mit uns per E-Mail in Verbindung zu setzen.	*If you need any further information, do not hesitate to contact us by e-mail.*
Besuchen Sie unsere Webseite.	*Why not visit our web site?*

WICHTIGE ABKÜRZUNGEN

a / c	account	Konto
am	ante meridiem	morgens; vormittags
asap	as soon as possible	so bald wie möglich
Assn	Association	Verband
attn.	(for the) attention (of)	zu Händen von (z. Hd.)
B / E	bill of exchange	Wechsel
B / L	bill of lading	Frachtbrief
cc	copy to, copies	Kopie an
cf.	compare	vergleichen
cfr	cost and freight	Kosten und Fracht
CGT	capital gains tax	Kapitalertragssteuer
cif	cost, insurance and freight	Kosten, Versicherung und Fracht
cip	carriage and insurance paid to	frachtfrei versichert
CIS	Commonwealth of Independent States	Gemeinschaft Unabhängiger Staaten (GUS)
C / N	credit note	Gutschrift
Co	company	Firma, Gesellschaft (Fa.)
c / o	care of	zu Händen von
cod	cash on delivery	Zahlung gegen Nachnahme
Corp.	Corporation	Gesellschaft
cpt	carriage paid to	frachtfrei
CR	credit	Guthaben
cwo	cash with order	Bezahlung bei Bestellung
D / A	documents against acceptance	Dokumente gegen Akzept
DD	direct debit	Direktabbuchung
ddp	delivery duty paid	geliefert verzollt
ddu	delivery duty unpaid	geliefert unverzollt
deq	delivered ex quay	geliefert ab Kai / verzollt
des	delivered ex ship	geliefert ab Schiff
DN	debit note	Lastschriftanzeige

D / P	documents against payment	Dokumente gegen Kasse
eg	for example	zum Beispiel
enc(s)	enclosure(s)	Anlage(n)
EXW	ex works	ab Werk
fao	for the attention of	zu Händen von
fas	free alongside ship	frei Längsseite Schiff
fca	free carrier	frei Frachtführer
fob	free on board	frei Schiff, frei an Bord
for	free on rail	frei Bahn
gr.	gross	brutto
HO	Head Office	Hauptniederlassung
ie	(Latin: id est) that is to say	das heißt (d.h.)
IMO	international money order	internationale Postanweisung
Inc	Incorporated (US)	amtlich (als Aktiengesellschaft) eingetragen
lb	pound	Pfund (engl. Pfund = 454 g)
L / C	letter of credit	Akkreditiv
Ltd	limited	(Gesellschaft) mit beschränkter Haftung
N / A	not applicable	entfällt
NB	Note (nota bene)	Merkzeichen, übrigens
NCV	no commercial value	ohne Handels- / Marktwert
no.	number	Nummer, Nr.
oz	ounce (weight)	Unze (Gewicht)
pa	per year (per annum)	pro Jahr
p & p	postage and packing	Porto und Verpackung
PLC	public limited company	Aktiengesellschaft
pm	post meridiem	nachmittags, abends
PO	Post Office; postal order	Postamt; Postanweisung
p.p.	(Latin: per procurationem) on behalf of	in Vertretung
pto	please turn over	bitte wenden (b.w.)
re	with reference to, regarding	bezüglich

Ref:	reference	Betreff; betrifft (betr.) (Briefkopf)
rlwy	railway	(Eisen-)Bahn
RRP	recommended retail price	unverbindliche Preisempfehlung, empfohlener Richtpreis
RSVP	(French: Répondez s'il vous plaît) please reply	um Antwort wird gebeten
SAE	stamped addressed envelope	frankierter Rückumschlag
VAT	Value Added Tax	Mehrwersteuer
wk	week	Woche
ZIP (code)	zone of improved delivery (US)	Postleitzahl

GLOSSAR ENGLISCH-DEUTSCH

(AE) = American English, (BE) = British English

A

abroad – im Ausland
accessories – Zubehör(-teile)
accommodation – Unterkunft
accordance (in ~ with) – in Übereinstimmung mit; gemäß
account – Konto
accountancy – Rechnungswesen, Buchhaltung
accountant – Buchhalter(in); Wirtschaftsprüfer(in)
accounting error – Buchungsfehler
accounts department – Rechnungsabteilung
accrue (to) – anfallen, -sammeln, -wachsen
acknowledge (to) – anerkennen; zugeben; bestätigen
acknowledge (to ~ receipt) – den Empfang bestätigen
acknowledgement (of receipt) – (Empfangs-)Bestätigung
act – Gesetz, Rechtshandlung
added value – Mehrwert
address – Adresse, Anschrift
addressee – Empfänger
adjourn (to) – verschieben, vertagen
adjustment – Anpassung; Regulierung
admit (to) – zugeben
advance (in ~) – im Voraus
advance payment – Vorauszahlung
advertisement – Annonce, Anzeige
advertising – Werbung, Reklame
advice – Rat(-schlag); Benachrichtigung
advice of payment – Zahlungsmitteilung
advise (to) – (be-)raten; benachrichtigen
after-sales service – Kundendienst
agency agreement – Vertretervertrag

agent – Vertreter, Repräsentant
agreement – Übereinkunft; Abkommen
air freight – Luftfracht
air waybill – Luftfrachtbrief
amount – Betrag, Summe
amount due – fälliger Betrag
announce (to) – ankündigen
annual – alljährlich
answer phone – Anrufbeantworter
answering machine – Anrufbeantworter
apologize (to) – sich entschuldigen
apology – Entschuldigung
appalling service – miserabler Service
applicant – Bewerber(in)
application (form) – Bewerbung(-svordruck, -sunterlagen)
apply (to ~ for) – sich bewerben um
appointed agent – Bevollmächtigte(r), Repräsentant(in)
appointment – Verabredung, Termin; Ernennung, Anstellung
appropriate – passend, geeignet; angemessen
approval (on ~) – zur Ansicht
area – Gebiet, Gegend
arrange (to) – veranlassen, arrangieren
arranged (as ~) – wie vereinbart
arrangements (to make ~) – Vorbereitungen / Vorkehrungen treffen
as from – beginnend am, ab dem (Datum)
ascertain (to) – ermitteln, feststellen
attachment – angehängte Datei
attend (to) – teilnehmen; anwesend sein
attention – Aufmerksamkeit
auditor – Wirtschaftsprüfer(in)
availability – Verfügbarkeit
available – verfügbar

average – Durchschnitt; durchschnittlich

B

balance *(financial)* – Saldo, Guthaben
bank account – (Bank-)Konto
banker's draft – Bankwechsel, Bank-
scheck
bed, breakfast and evening meal –
Zimmer mit Halbpension
beneficial – vorteilhaft, nützlich
besides – außerdem, ferner
bid *(AE)* – Angebotsausschreibung
bill of exchange – Wechsel
bill of lading – Konnossement
blank cheque – Blankoscheck
block capitals – Blockschrift
book (to) – buchen, reservieren
booking – Reservierung
boom – Hochkonjunktur
branch – Filiale, Zweigstelle
brand – (Firmen-)Marke
breakages – Bruch, zerbrochene Ware
breakdown – Panne, technischer
Defekt
brisk trade – florierender Handel
broaden (to) – ausweiten, erweitern
browser – Browser
bulk – (große) Menge, Masse
business (on ~) – geschäftlich
buyer – Käufer
by *(e.g. air freight)* – per *(z. B.
Luftfracht)*

C

cancel (to) – absagen, streichen,
rückgängig machen
candidate – Kandidat(in); Bewerber(in)
capital letters – Großbuchstaben
cargo – Fracht
carriage free – frachtfrei
carriage paid – frei Haus
carrier – Spediteur
carry (to ~ out) – aus-, durchführen
cash advance – Barvorschuss
cash in advance – Vorauszahlung

cash on delivery – per Nachnahme /
Zahlung gegen Nachnahme
casual dress – zwanglose / legere
Kleidung
cater (to ~ to one's needs) – seine
Bedürfnisse befriedigen
certified true – beglaubigte Abschrift /
Kopie
cfr (cost and freight) – Kosten und
Fracht
chain of hotels – Hotelkette
chairman, -woman, -person –
Vorsitzende(r)
challenge – Herausforderung
charge (to) – berechnen
charges – Kosten
charges forward – Nachnahme,
Zahlung nach Warenerhalt
check (to) – prüfen
cif (cost, insurance and freight) –
Kosten, Versicherung, Fracht
cip (carriage and insurance paid to) –
frachtfrei versichert
claim – Anspruch; Forderung
clear (to ~ an account) – e. Konto
ausgleichen
clear (to ~ through customs) –
zollamtlich abfertigen
clerical error – Bearbeitungsfehler
come (to ~ across sth) – (zufällig) auf
etw stoßen
comment – Kommentar
commission (rate of ~) – Provision
company – Firma
compensation – Entschädigung
competition – Wettbewerb;
Konkurrenz
competitive – wettbewerbs-,
konkurrenzfähig
competitor – Konkurrent
complain (to) – sich beschweren
complaint – Beschwerde, Reklamation
comply (to ~ with sth) – e. Sache
entsprechen; in Einklang mit etw
stehen

components – Zubehör-, Einzelteile
concern (to whom it may ~) – an alle, die es betrifft
conditions – Bedingungen
condolences – Beileidswünsche
confident – sicher, zuversichtlich
confirm (to) – bestätigen
congratulate (to) – gratulieren
congratulations – Glückwünsche
connection – Verbindung, Beziehung
consignee – Empfänger, Adressat
consignment – Versand, Lieferung
consignor – Absender, Versender
construction equipment – Bau-maschinen
consumer – Verbraucher(in)
consumer boom – Hochkonjunktur
contact (to) – sich in Verbindung setzen mit
contact (to get in ~) – Kontakt aufnehmen
content – Inhalt
contract – Vertrag
convenience (at your earliest ~) – möglichst bald
convenient (to be ~) – bequem / passend / geeignet sein
copy – Kopie
courier (by ~) – per Eilboten
covered (to be ~ by insurance) – durch eine Versicherung gedeckt sein
cpt (carriage paid to) – frachtfrei
crate – (Fracht-)Kiste
create (to) your own web site – eine Internetseite erstellen
credit (to give ~) – Kredit gewähren
credit (to) – gutschreiben
credit facilities – Kreditmodalitäten
credit note – Gutschriftsanzeige
credit terms – Kreditbedingungen
creditor – Gläubiger
currency – Währung
current – laufend; momentan
curriculum vitae – Lebenslauf

custom (thank you for your ~) – wir bedanken uns für die gute Zusammenarbeit
customer – Kunde, Kundin
customs – Zoll(polizei)
customs clearance – Zollabfertigung
customs duties – Zollgebühren

D

daf (delivered at frontier) – geliefert Grenze
damaged – beschädigt
damages – Schäden
ddp (delivered duty paid) – geliefert verzollt
ddu (delivered duty unpaid) – geliefert unverzollt
deadline – Stichtag, letzter Termin
deal (to ~ with) – (be)handeln, sich befassen mit
dealer – Händler(in)
debit – Soll, Lastschrift
debit (to) – (Konto) belasten, debitieren
debt(s) – Schulden
deduct (to) – abziehen
defect – Defekt, Schaden
defective – defekt, fehlerhaft
delay – Verzögerung
delay (to) – verzögern
deliver (to) – (aus)liefern
delivery – Auslieferung
delivery (to take ~ of) – in Empfang nehmen
delivery duty paid – geliefert verzollt
delivery slip – Lieferschein
demand – Forderung
department – Abteilung
depleted stocks – erschöpfte Vorräte
deposit account – Sparkonto
deq (delivered ex quay) – geliefert ab Kai, verzollt
des (delivered ex ship) – geliefert ab Schiff

despatch (to) *(also dispatch)* – abfertigen, abschicken
detail (to) – einzeln aufführen
details – Einzelheiten
dial (to) in – sich einwählen
direct debit – Direktabbuchung
discount – Preisnachlass, Rabatt
discrepancy – Abweichung, Unstimmigkeit
disembark (to) – ausladen, löschen
dispatch *(also despatch)* – Abfertigung, Versand
dispatch (to) *(also despatch)* – abfertigen, abschicken
display (on ~) – ausgestellt
display (to) – ausstellen
disruption – Störung
distressed (to be ~) – bekümmert / unglücklich sein
distribution company – Vertriebsgesellschaft
DIY (Do It Yourself) products – Heimwerkerprodukte
documents against payment – Dokumente gegen Zahlung
download (to) – herunterladen
draft – Wechsel
draw (to ~ out money) – Geld abheben
draw (to ~ so's attention to sth) – jdn auf etw hinweisen
driving licence – Führerschein (BE)
driver's license – Führerschein (AE)
due date – Fälligkeitstermin
duly signed – ordnungsgemäß unterzeichnet
duplicate – Doppel, Duplikat
dutiable – abgaben-, zollpflichtig
duty free – zollfrei
duty paid – verzollt

E

electronic correspondence – elektronische Korrespondenz
e-mail address – E-Mail-Adresse

emphasize (to) – betonen
enclose (to) – beifügen
enclosed – anbei, (in der) Anlage
engineer – Ingenieur(in)
enquire (to) *(also inquire)* – sich erkundigen, fragen
enquiry *(also inquiry)* – Anfrage
envelope – Umschlag
estate car – Kombi(-wagen)
estimate – Schätzung; Kostenvoranschlag
estimate (to) – schätzen
evaluation – Bewertung
evening dress – Abendkleidung
exceed (to) – übersteigen
exchange rate – Wechselkurs
exclusively – exklusiv; ausschließlich
execute (to ~ an order) – e. Auftrag ausführen
exhibit (to) – ausstellen
exhibition – Ausstellung
expenses – Spesen, Ausgaben
extension of payment time – Zahlungsaufschub
extension wire – Verlängerungskabel
extra cost (to charge at ~~) – zuzüglich berechnen
ex works – ab Werk, ab Lager, ab Fabrik

F

factory – Fabrik, Werk
fail (to ~ to do sth) – versäumen etw zu tun
failure to pay – Zahlungsunfähigkeit
fair – Messe
favo(u)rites – Favoriten
fca (free carrier) – frei Frachtführer
fee – Gebühr, Honorar
field (in the ~ of) – auf dem Gebiet / im Bereich von
file – Akte
file (to) – ablegen
financial standing / status – Finanzlage

financial year – Wirtschafts-, Haushaltsjahr
fine – Strafe
firm – Firma, Gesellschaft
firm offer – verbindliches Angebot
fluent (to be ~ in a language) – fließend e. Sprache sprechen
following – (nach-)folgend
force (in ~) – rechtskräftig, gültig
form – Formular
formal dress – Gesellschaftskleidung
forthcoming – baldig, bevorstehend
forward (to) – nachschicken, weiterleiten
forward (to) a mail – eine Nachricht / Mail weiterleiten
forwarding address – Nachsendeadresse
forwarding agent – Spediteur
free carrier – frei Frachtführer
free of charge (frc) – kostenlos, umsonst
free on board (fob) – frei Schiff
freight or carriage paid to... – frachtfrei
freight, carriage and insurance paid to... – frachtfrei versichert
fulfil (to ~ a requirement) – eine Anforderung erfüllen
full board – Vollpension
fully booked – belegt
funds – Mittel, Gelder
further – weiter, ferner; zusätzlich

G
gain (to ~ experience) – Erfahrung(en) sammeln
gateway – Gateway
goods – Ware(n)
graduate (to) – einen (akademischen) Grad erlangen; die Abschlussprüfung ablegen
grant (to ~ a discount) – einen Rabatt gewähren

grateful (to be ~) – dankbar sein
guarantee (to) – garantieren
guarantor – Bürge, Bürgin

H
half board – Halbpension
handling charge – Bearbeitungsgebühr; Umladekosten; Kontoführungsgebühr
harbour – Hafen
have (to ~ sth on) – etw vorhaben
head office – Zentrale, Hauptverwaltung
hereafter – nachfolgend, von jetzt an
hereby – hiermit
hermetically sealed – hermetisch versiegelt
high standard – hohes Niveau, hohe Qualität
hire (to) – mieten
hospitality – Gastfreundschaft

I
import (to) files – Dateien importieren
importer – Importeur, Importfirma
improve (to) – verbessern
in-house – hausintern, innerbetrieblich
inadequate packing – unsachgemäße Verpackung
included – inbegriffen
including – inklusive
inclusive – einschließlich
inconvenience – Unannehmlichkeit
increase – Wachstum, Steigerung
increase (to) – zunehmen, ansteigen
incur (to ~ expenses) – Unkosten haben
inform (to) – informieren
initial order – Erstbestellung
inlaid *(e.g. with diamonds)* – eingearbeitet *(z. B. mit Brillanten)*
inquire (to) *(also enquire)* – sich erkundigen, fragen
inquiry *(also enquiry)* – Anfrage

installation – Installation; Anschluss; Einbau

instalment (monthly ~) – Monatsrate

instructions for use – Gebrauchsanweisung

insurance – Versicherung

insurance (to take out an ~ policy) – e. Versicherung abschließen

insurer – Versicherer

intend (to ~ to do sth) – planen / vorhaben etw zu tun

intermediary – Mittelsperson

Internet access – Internet-Zugang

Internet user – Internetbenutzer(in)

interview – (Einstellungs-)Gespräch

introductory price – Einführungspreis

investigation (upon ~) – bei näherer Untersuchung

invoice – Rechnung

invoice (to) – in Rechnung stellen, berechnen

K

keep (to ~ an appointment) – eine Verabredung einhalten

kind – nett, freundlich

kindness – Freundlichkeit

L

launching – Einführung (e. Produkts)

leaflet – Broschüre

legal department – Rechtsabteilung

letter of credit (L / C) – Akkreditiv

liability – Haftung

liable – haftbar

link – Verbindung, Beziehung

loading – Be-, Verladen

lobby – Foyer

look (to ~ forward to) – sich freuen auf

loss – Verlust

lot – Partie, Posten

M

mail *(AE)* – Post

mail (to forward a ~) – eine Nachricht / Mail weiterleiten

mail (to receive a ~) – eine Nachricht / Mail empfangen

mail (to send a ~) – eine Nachricht / Mail senden

mailbox – elektronisches Postfach

maintenance engineer – Wartungsingenieur(in)

management – Geschäftsführung, -leitung

manufacturer – Hersteller(in)

manufacturing plant – Fabrik, Produktionsstätte

manufacturing process – Herstellung (-svorgang)

market – Markt

maturity date – Fälligkeit(-stermin)

measure (to) – messen

meet (to) – treffen

meet (to ~ a deadline) – einen Termin einhalten

meeting – Treffen, Versammlung

mention (to) – erwähnen

mentioned (as ~) – wie … erwähnt

merger – Fusion

message pad – Notizblock

mistake – Fehler

misunderstanding – Missverständnis

model – Modell

money order – Geldanweisung

N

negotiate (to) – verhandeln über

net price – Nettopreis

network – Netz(-werk)

note – Notiz, Vermerk

note (to) – bemerken; zur Kenntnis nehmen

notice – Notiz

notify (to) – benachrichtigen

O

obliged – gezwungen; dankbar, verbunden

occasion – Gelegenheit
occur (to) – sich ereignen, passieren
office – Büro
opportunity – (günstige) Gelegenheit
opportunity (to take the ~ to) – die Gelegenheit ergreifen(,) zu
optional – auf Wunsch erhältlich; freiwillig; fakultativ
optional extras – Extras
order – Bestellung, Auftrag
order (to) – bestellen
order cheque – Orderscheck
order form – Bestellformular
outskirts – (äußere) Vororte, Stadtrand
outstanding – ausstehend, unerledigt; hervorragend
overbook (to) – überbelegen, überbuchen
overdraft – (Konto-)Überziehung
overdrawn – überzogen (Konto)
overdue – überfällig
overseas – in / nach Übersee; *(in GB auch:)* in / nach Europa
owing to – wegen, aufgrund

P

package tour – Pauschalreise
packing – Verpackung
particulars – Einzelheiten
partnership – Partnerschaft
patronage – Schirmherrschaft, Unterstützung; Vertrauen, Treue
payable by you – geht zu Ihren Lasten
per (as ~) – gemäß, laut
performance – Leistung
place (to ~ an order) – eine Bestellung aufgeben
plan (to ~ to do sth) – planen / vorhaben, etw zu tun
plenty of – viel, e. Menge
popular – beliebt
possible (as soon as ~) – so bald wie möglich
post – Post; Stelle

post (to) – mit der Post schicken, abschicken
postcode – Postleitzahl
postpone (to) – verschieben
potential – potenziell
preferential rate – Sonderpreis
premises – Geschäftsräume, Anwesen
previous – vorhergehend
price list – Preisliste
prior – vorausgehend, früher
prior notice – vorherige Benachrichtigung
prior sale – Zwischenverkauf
private – persönlich *(auf Briefen)*
pro forma invoice – Proforma-Rechnung
proceedings (to take ~) – gerichtlich vorgehen, einen Prozess anstrengen
process (to) – behandeln, verarbeiten
product line – Produktlinie, Kollektion
profit margin – Profitspanne
promising – viel versprechend
promotion – Beförderung; Werbeveranstaltung
proposal – Vorschlag
propose (to) – vorschlagen
provider – Anbieter
purchase – Kauf
put off (to) *(informal)* – verschieben; hinausschieben

Q

quarter – Vierteljahr
quarterly – vierteljährlich
query – Frage, Problem
query (to) – um e. Überprüfung / Erklärung bitten
quotation – Kostenvoranschlag, Preisangebot
quote (to ~ a price) – e. Preis angeben

R

rail (by ~) – per Bahn
range – Reihe, Sortiment
rate – Preis, Tarif

raw material – Rohmaterial
ready for despatch – fertig zur Auslieferung
receive (to) a mail – eine Nachricht / Mail empfangen
receipt – Empfang, Erhalt; Quittung
receiver *(Telefon)* – Hörer
recently – kürzlich, vor kurzem
reception – Empfang
recipient – Empfänger
recommend (to) – empfehlen
recovery – Erholung, Genesung
recruit (to) – ein-, anstellen, anwerben
referee – Referenz
reference (with ~ to) – mit Bezug auf, bezüglich
refund (to) – (zurück-)erstatten
regarding – bezüglich
regards (as ~) – was … betrifft
registered letter – eingeschriebener Brief
registered (by ~ post) – per Einschreiben
regulation – Regelung, Regulierung
reimbursement – Rückerstattung
reliable – verlässlich
remind (to ~ sb) – jdn erinnern
reminder – Erinnerung
remittance – Überweisung
renew (to) – erneuern, verlängern
rent (to) – mieten
repeat order – Nachbestellung
replace (to) – ersetzen
replacement – Ersatz
reply – Antwort
reply (in ~ to your) – in Beantwortung (Ihres / Ihrer)
report – Bericht, Gutachten
representative – Repräsentant(in), Vertreter(in)
request (on ~) – auf Anfrage
request (to) – bitten, nachsuchen
requirement – Anforderung, Bedingung
reserve (to) – reservieren (lassen)

respite – Zahlungsaufschub
retail (to) – im Einzelhandel verkaufen
retail price – Ladenpreis
retailer – Einzelhändler(in)
retire (to) – in Pension gehen; ausscheiden aus
return (to) – zurückgeben, -schicken
return address – Absender(-adresse)
return (by ~ of post) – postwendend
return flight – Rückflug; Hin- und Rückflug
return to sender – zurück an den Absender
reward – Belohnung

S

sales manager – Verkaufsleiter(in)
sales – Verkäufe
sales department – Vertrieb, Verkaufsabteilung
sales policy – Verkaufsstrategie
sales representative – (Handels-) Vertreter(in)
salesman, -woman – Verkäufer(in)
sample – Muster
satisfy (to ~ a requirement) – einer Anforderung entsprechen
savings account – Sparkonto
schedule – Zeitplan
seat – (Sitz-)Platz
send (to) – schicken
send (to) a mail – eine Nachricht / Mail senden
sender – Absender
separate (under ~ cover) – mit getrennter Post
service (to be of ~ to sb) – jdm nützen
settle (to) – regeln
settlement – Bezahlung; Ausgleich
shareware – Shareware
ship (to) – verschiffen
shipment – Warensendung; Verschiffung
short-listed (to be ~) – in die engere Wahl kommen

show (to) – vorstellen, präsentieren
sight bill – Sichtwechsel
sight draft – Sichtwechsel
sign (to) – unterzeichnen, -schreiben
single flight – Einfachflug
single room – Einzelzimmer
single ticket – Einzelfahrschein, -karte
slight – leicht; unwesentlich
snail mail – üblicher Postweg
sold out – ausverkauft
sole agent – Alleinvertreter(in)
spare parts – Ersatzteile
specification sheet – Spezifikation; technische Beschreibung
specify (to) – genau angeben
stand – (Messe-)Stand; Untergestell *(für Telefon)*
standard – Norm; Maßstab; Niveau; Standard
standard *(adj)* – üblich, Standard-, Normal-
standard charges – Standardpreise
starting salary – Anfangsgehalt
statement of account – Kontoauszug; Abrechnung
steps (to take ~) – Maßnahmen ergreifen
stipulate (to) – verlangen; festsetzen; fordern
stock (in ~) – vorrätig
stock (to have sth in ~) – etw vorrätig haben
stock (to) – am Lager führen
storage – (Ein-)Lagerung
storage (in ~) – auf Lager
store (to) – lagern, (EDV) ablegen
strike – Streik
strive (to ~ to do sth) – bemüht sein etw zu tun
subject to – abhängig von, vorbehaltlich
submit (to) – vorlegen; einreichen
subsequent order – Folgebestellung
subsidiary – Nebenstelle, Filiale
subscribe (to) – abonnieren

substantially reduced – großzügig reduziert
substitute – Ersatz
suggest (to) – vorschlagen
suit (to) – passen
suitable – passend; geeignet
sum – Summe
supplier – Lieferant(in)
supply (to) – (be-)liefern
surf (to) the Internet – im Internet herumstöbern
survey of damage – Schadensaufnahme

T

tally (to) – übereinstimmen *(Zahlen, Berichte)*
technical adviser – technische(r) Berater(in)
technical specifications – technische Angaben
tender *(BE)* – Angebotsausschreibung
terms – Bedingungen
terms of payment – Zahlungsbedingungen
throughout – die ganze Zeit über; überall in
together with – zusammen mit, sowie
touch (to get in ~ with so) – sich bei jdm melden
trade fair – Handelsmesse
trading company – Handelsgesellschaft
training – Ausbildung
transfer (bank ~) – Banküberweisung
trial – Versuch
trip – Reise
turnover – Umsatz
typing error – Tippfehler

U

underline (to) – unterstreichen
undermentioned – unten erwähnt
underwriter – Versicherer
unfortunate – bedauerlich

unfortunately – leider
unit price – Preis pro Einheit, Stückpreis
unload (to) – ausladen
unloading – Entladen, Löschen
unsaleable – unverkäuflich
unsatisfactory – unbefriedigend
unsubscribe (to) – Abo kündigen
updated – auf den neuesten Stand gebracht
utmost urgency – äußerste Dringlichkeit

V

vacancies (no ~) – belegt
vacancy – freie Stelle; (leeres) Zimmer
vacant – unbesetzt; leer; frei
valid – gültig
value – Wert
visit (to) – besuchen

W

warehouse – Lager(-haus)
warrant – Bescheinigung; Vollmacht
web site – Webseite
waybill – Frachtbrief
weigh (to) – wiegen
well (as ~ as) – sowohl ... als auch
whether – ob
wholesale – Großhandel
wholesaler – Großhändler(in)
wide – umfassend; weit
wishes (best ~) – herzliche Glückwünsche
within a week – innerhalb e. Woche
wonder (to) – sich fragen

Z

zipped file – komprimierte (gezippte) datei

GLOSSAR DEUTSCH-ENGLISCH

(AE) = American English, (BE) = British English

A

ab dem *(Datum)* – as from
Abendkleidung – evening dress
abfertigen – to dispatch / despatch
abfertigen (zollamtlich ~) – to clear through customs
Abfertigung – dispatch / despatch
abgabenpflichtig – dutiable
abhängig von – independent of; subject to
abheben (Geld ~) – to draw out money
Abkommen – agreement
ablegen – to store, file
Abo kündigen – to unsubscribe
abonnieren – to subscribe
Abrechnung – statement; invoice
absagen – to cancel
abschicken – to dispatch / despatch; to post
Abschlussprüfung (die ~ ablegen) – to graduate
Absender – consignor, sender
Absenderadresse – return address
Abteilung – department
Abweichung – discrepancy
abziehen – to deduct
Adressat – consignee
Adresse – address
Akkreditiv – letter of credit
Akte – file
Alleinvertreter(in) – sole agent
alljährlich – annual
an alle, die es betrifft – to whom it may concern
anbei – enclosed
Anbieter – provider
anfallen *(z. B. Zinsen)* – to accrue *(e.g. interest)*
Anfangsgehalt – starting salary

Anforderung – requirement
Anforderung (e. ~ erfüllen) – to fulfil a requirement
Anfrage – inquiry / enquiry *(BE)*
Anfrage (auf ~) – upon / on request
Angaben (technische ~) – technical specifications
Angebotsausschreibung – tender *(BE)*, bid *(AE)*
angehängte Datei – attachment
ankündigen – to announce
Anlage (in der ~) – enclosed
Annonce – advertisement
Anpassung – adjustment
Anrufbeantworter – answer phone; answering machine
Anschluss – installation
Anschrift – address
Ansicht (zur ~) – on approval
Anspruch – claim
ansteigen – to increase
anstellen – to recruit
Antwort – reply
anwachsen – to accrue
anwerben – to recruit
Anwesen – premises
anwesend sein – to attend, be present
Anzeige – advertisement
arrangieren – to arrange
aufführen (einzeln ~) – to detail
aufgeben (e. Bestellung ~) – to place an order
aufgrund – owing to
Aufmerksamkeit – attention
Auftrag – order
Ausbildung – training
ausführen – to carry out
ausführen (e. Auftrag ~) – to execute an order
Ausgaben – expenses

ausgestellt – on display

ausgleichen (e. Konto ~) – to clear an account

ausladen – to unload, disembark

Ausland (im ~) – abroad

ausliefern – to deliver

Auslieferung – delivery

ausscheiden aus – to retire

ausschließlich – exclusively

außerdem – besides

ausstehend – outstanding

ausstellen – to display, exhibit

Ausstellung – exhibition

ausverkauft – sold out

ausweiten – to broaden

B

Bahn (per ~) – by rail

baldig – forthcoming

Bankkonto – bank account

Banküberweisung – bank transfer

Bankwechsel – banker's draft

Barvorschuss – cash advance

Baumaschinen – construction equipment

Beantwortung (in ~ Ihres / Ihrer ...) – in reply to your...

Bearbeitungsfehler – clerical error

Bearbeitungsgebühr – handling charge

bedauerlich – unfortunate

Bedingung – requirement; condition, term

Bedürfnisse (seine ~ befriedigen) – to cater to one's needs

befassen (sich ~ mit) – to deal with

Beförderung – promotion *(job)*

beginnend am *(Datum)* – as from

beglaubigte Abschrift / Kopie – certified true

behandeln – to deal with, process

beifügen – to enclose

Beileidswünsche – condolences

bekümmert sein – to be distressed

Beladen – loading

belasten (e. Konto ~) – to debit an account

belegt – fully booked, no vacancies

beliebt – popular

beliefern – to supply

Belohnung – reward

bemerken – to note, notice

bemüht sein etw zu tun – to strive to do sth

benachrichtigen – to inform, notify, advise

Benachrichtigung – notification, advice

beraten – to advise

berechnen – to charge; to invoice

Bereich (im ~ von) – in the field of

Bericht – report

beschädigt – damaged

Bescheinigung – warrant

Beschwerde – complaint

beschweren (sich ~) – to complain

bestätigen – to confirm; to acknowledge *(receipt)*

Bestätigung (Empfangs~) – acknowledgement of receipt

bestellen – to order

Bestellformular – order form

Bestellung – order

Bestellung (e. ~ aufgeben) – to place an order

besuchen – to visit

betonen – to emphasize

Betrag – amount, sum

betrifft (was ... ~) – as regards

Bevollmächtigte(r) – appointed agent

bevorstehend – forthcoming

bewerben (sich ~ um) – to apply for

Bewerber(in) – applicant, candidate

Bewerbungsvordruck – application form

Bewertung – evaluation

Beziehung – connection, relation

Bezug (mit ~ auf) – with reference to

bezüglich – with reference to, regarding

bitten – to ask, request
Blankoscheck – blank cheque
Blockschrift – block capitals
Broschüre – booklet, leaflet
Browser – browser
Bruch – breakages
buchen – to book
Buchhalter(in) – accountant
Buchhaltung – accountancy
Buchungsfehler – accounting error
Bürge, Bürgin – guarantor
Büro – office

D
dankbar sein – to be grateful
Datei (gezippte ~) – (zipped) file
debitieren – to debit
Defekt – defect
defekt – defective
Direktabbuchung – direct debit
Direktion – directorate; head office
Dokumente gegen Zahlung – documents against payment
Doppel – duplicate, copy
Dringlichkeit (äußerste ~) – utmost urgency
Duplikat – duplicate
durchführen – to carry out
Durchschnitt – average
durchschnittlich – average

E
Eilboten (per ~) – by courier
Einfachflug – single flight
Einführung *(e. Produkts)* – launching
Einführungspreis – introductory price
eingearbeitet *(z. B. mit Brillanten)* – inlaid *(e.g. with diamonds)*
eingeschriebener Brief – registered letter
einhalten (e. Termin ~) – to meet a deadline
Einklang (in ~ mit etw stehen) – to comply with
Einlagerung – storage

einreichen – to submit
einschließlich – inclusive
Einschreiben (per ~) – by registered post
einstellen – to recruit
Einstellungsgespräch – interview
einwählen (sich ~) – to dial in
Einzelfahrkarte – single ticket
Einzelfahrschein – single ticket
Einzelhandel (im ~ verkaufen) – to retail
Einzelhändler(in) – retailer
Einzelheiten – details, particulars
Einzelteile – component parts
Einzelzimmer – single room
elektronische Korrespondenz – electronic correspondence
elektronisches Postfach – mailbox
E-Mail-Adresse – e-mail address
Empfang – reception; receipt
Empfang (den ~ bestätigen) – to acknowledge receipt
Empfang (in ~ nehmen) – to take delivery of
Empfänger – addressee, consignee, recipient
empfehlen – to recommend
Entladen – unloading
Entschädigung – compensation
entschuldigen (sich ~) – to apologize
Entschuldigung – apology
entsprechen (e. Anforderung ~) – to satisfy a requirement
entsprechen (e. Sache ~) – to comply with
entstehen – to arise; to result
ereignen (sich ~) – to occur
Erfahrung(en) sammeln – to gain experience
Erhalt – receipt
Erholung – recovery
erinnern (jdn ~) – to remind sb
Erinnerung – reminder
Erklärung (um e. ~bitten) – to query

erkundigen (sich ~) – to inquire / enquire
ermitteln – to ascertain
Ernennung – appointment
erneuern – to renew
Ersatz – substitute, replacement
Ersatzteile – spare parts
erschöpfte Vorräte – depleted stocks
ersetzen – to replace
Erstbestellung – initial order
erwähnen – to mention
erweitern – to broaden
exklusiv – exclusive
Export – export
Extras – optional extras

F

Fabrik – factory, manufacturing plant
Fabrik (ab ~) – ex works
fälliger Betrag – amount due
Fälligkeitstermin – due / maturity date
Favoriten – favo(u)rites
Fehler – mistake
fehlerhaft – defective
ferner – besides
fertig zur Auslieferung – ready for dispatch / despatch
festsetzen – to stipulate
feststellen – to ascertain
Filiale – branch, subsidiary
Finanzlage – financial standing / status
Firma – company, firm
Firmenmarke – brand
fließend e. Sprache sprechen – to be fluent in a language
florierender Handel – brisk trade
Folgebestellung – subsequent order
fordern – to stipulate
Forderung – demand; claim
Formular – form
Foyer – lobby
Fracht – freight, cargo
Frachtbrief – waybill
frachtfrei – cpt (carriage paid to)

frachtfrei versichert – cip (carriage and insurance paid to)
Frage – question; query
fragen – to ask, inquire / enquire
fragen (sich ~) – to wonder
frei – free, vacant
frei Frachtführer – fca (free carrier)
frei Schiff – fob (free on board)
freuen (sich ~ auf) – to look forward to
freundlich – kind
Freundlichkeit – kindness
früher – prior
Führerschein – driving licence (BE), – driver's license (AE)
Fusion – merger

G

garantieren – to guarantee
Gateway – gateway
Gastfreundschaft – hospitality
Gebiet – area
Gebiet (auf dem ~ von) – in the field of
Gebrauchsanweisung – instructions for use
Gebühr – fee
geeignet – appropriate; suitable; convenient
Gegend – area
Geldanweisung – money order
Gelder – funds
Gelegenheit – opportunity, occasion
Gelegenheit (die ~ ergreifen, zu) – to take the opportunity to
geliefert ab Kai / verzollt – deq (delivered ex quay)
geliefert ab Schiff – des (delivered ex ship)
geliefert ab Grenze – daf (delivered at frontier)
geliefert unverzollt – ddu (delivered duty unpaid)
geliefert verzollt – ddp (delivered duty paid)
gemäß – in accordance with, as per

genau angeben – to specify
Genesung – recovery
gerichtlich vorgehen – to take (legal) proceedings
geschäftlich – on business
Geschäftsführung – management
Geschäftsräume – premises
Gesellschaft – firm, company
Gesellschaftskleidung – formal dress
Gesetz – law; act
Gespräch – conversation; interview
getrennt (mit ~er Post) – under separate cover
gezwungen – obliged
Gläubiger – creditor
Glückwünsche (herzliche ~) – many congratulations, best wishes
Grad (e. akademischen ~ erlangen) – to graduate
gratulieren – to congratulate
Großbuchstaben – capital letters
Großhandel – wholesale
Großhändler(in) – wholesaler
großzügig reduziert – substantially reduced
gültig – in force, valid
Gutachten – report
Guthaben – balance
gutschreiben – to credit
Gutschriftsanzeige – credit note

H
Hafen – harbour
haftbar – liable
Haftung – liability
Halbpension – half board
Halbpension (Zimmer mit ~) – bed, breakfast and evening meal
Handelsgesellschaft – trading company
Handelsmesse – trade fair
Handelsvertreter(in) – sales representative
Händler(in) – trader, dealer
Hauptverwaltung – head office

Haus (frei ~) – carriage paid
Haushaltsjahr – financial year
hausintern – in-house
Heimwerkerprodukte – DIY (Do It Yourself) products
Herausforderung – challenge
hermetisch versiegelt – hermetically sealed
Hersteller(in) – manufacturer
Herstellung, -svorgang – manufacturing process
herunterladen – to download
hiermit – hereby
hinausschieben – to put off *(informal)*
Hinflug – outward *(BE)* outgoing *(AE)* flight
Hin- und Rückflug – return flight
hinweisen (jdn auf etw ~) – to draw sb's attention to sth
Hochkonjunktur – (consumer) boom
Honorar – fees
Hörer – receiver *(Telefon)*
Hotelkette – chain of hotels

I
Importeur – importer
Importfirma – importer
importieren (Dateien ~) – to import (files)
inbegriffen – included
informieren – to inform
Ingenieur(in) – engineer
Inhalt – content
inklusive – including
innerbetrieblich – in-house
innerhalb e. Woche – within a week
Installation – installation
Internet (im ~ rumstöbern) – to surf the Internet
Internetbenutzer(in) – Internet user
Internetseite (eine ~ erstellen) – to create your own web site

J
jetzt (von ~ an) – hereafter

K

Kandidat(in) – candidate
Kauf – purchase
Käufer – buyer
Kenntnis (zur ~ nehmen) – to note
Kiste – crate
Kollektion – product line
Kombi(-wagen) – estate car
Kommentar – comment
Kommissionssatz – rate of commission
komprimierte Datei – zipped file
Konkurrent – competitor
Konkurrenz – competition
konkurrenzfähig – competitive
Konnossement – bill of lading
Kontakt aufnehmen – to get in contact
Konto – account
Kontoauszug – statement of account
Kontoführungsgebühr – handling charge
Kontoüberziehung – overdraft
Kopie – copy
Kosten – costs; expenses; charges
Kosten und Fracht – cfr (cost and freight)
Kosten, Versicherung, Fracht – cif (cost, insurance, freight)
kostenlos – free of charge
Kostenvoranschlag – quotation; estimate
Kredit gewähren – to give credit
Kreditbedingungen – credit terms
Kreditmodalitäten – credit facilities
Kunde, Kundin – customer
Kundendienst – after-sales service
kurzem (vor ~) – recently
kürzlich – recently

L

Ladenpreis – retail price
Lager (am ~ führen) – to stock
Lager (auf ~) – in storage
Lager(-haus) – warehouse
lagern – to store
Lagerung – storage

Lasten (geht zu Ihren ~) – payable by you
Lastschrift – debit
laufend – current
laut – according to
Lebenslauf – curriculum vitae
leer – empty, vacant
legere Kleidung – casual dress
leicht – slight; easy
leider – unfortunately
Leistung – performance
letzter Termin – deadline
Lieferant(in) – supplier
liefern – to supply; to deliver
Lieferschein – delivery slip
löschen – to unload, disembark
Luftfracht – air freight
Luftfrachtbrief – air waybill

M

Mail (eine ~ empfangen) – to receive a mail
Mail (eine ~ senden) – to send a mail
Mail (eine ~ weiterleiten) – to forward a mail
Markt – market
Maßnahmen ergreifen – to take steps
Maßstab – standard
Mehrwert – added value
melden (sich bei jdm ~) – to get in touch with sb
Menge (e. ~) – plenty of
Menge (große ~) – bulk
Messe – fair
messen – to measure
mieten – to hire; to rent
miserabler Service – appalling service
Missverständnis – misunderstanding
Mittel – funds
Mittelsperson – intermediary
Modell – model
möglich (so bald wie ~) – as soon as possible
möglichst bald – at your earliest convenience

Monatsrate – monthly instalment
Muster – sample

N

Nachbestellung – repeat order
nachfolgend – following; hereafter
Nachnahme (per ~ / Zahlung gegen ~) – cash on delivery
Nachricht (eine ~ empfangen) – to receive a mail
Nachricht (eine ~ senden) – to send a mail
Nachricht (eine ~ weiterleiten) – to forward a mail
nachschicken – to forward
Nachsendeadresse – forwarding address
nachsuchen – to request
Nebenstelle – subsidiary
nett – kind, nice
Nettopreis – net price
Netz(-werk) – network
Niveau – level; standard
Norm – norm; standard
Normal- – standard
Notiz – note
Notizblock – message pad
nützen (jdm ~) – to be of service to sb
nützlich – beneficial

O

ob – if; whether
Orderscheck – order cheque
ordnungsgemäß unterzeichnet – duly signed

P

Panne – breakdown
Partie – part; lot, batch
Partnerschaft – partnership
passen – to suit
passend – appropriate; suitable; convenient
passieren – to happen, occur
Pauschalreise – package tour

Pension (in ~ gehen) – to retire
per *(z. B. Luftfracht)* – by *(e.g. air freight)*
persönlich *(auf Briefen)* – private
planen etw zu tun – to plan to do sth
Platz – seat
Post – post *(BE)*, mail *(AE)*
Posten – post, position; quantity, lot
Postleitzahl – postcode
Postweg (üblicher ~) – snail mail
postwendend – by return of post
potenziell – potential
präsentieren – to show
Präsident(in) – President; chairman, -woman
Preis – price; rate
Preis (e. ~ angeben) – to quote a price
Preis pro Einheit – unit price
Preisangebot – quotation
Preisliste – price list
Preisnachlass – discount
Problem – problem; query
Produktionsstätte – manufacturing plant
Produktlinie – product line
Profitspanne – profit margin
Proformarechnung – pro forma invoice
Prozess (e. ~ anstrengen) – to take (legal) proceedings
prüfen – to check

Q

Qualität (hohe ~) – high standard
Quittung – receipt

R

Rabatt – discount
Rabatt (e. ~ gewähren) – to grant a discount
Rat(-schlag) – advice
Rechnung – invoice
Rechnung (in ~ stellen) – to invoice

Rechnungsabteilung – accounts department
Rechnungswesen – accountancy
Rechtsabteilung – legal department
Rechtshandlung – act
rechtskräftig – in force
Referenz – referee
regeln – to settle
Regelung – regulation
Regulierung – regulation, adjustment
Reihe – range
Reise – trip
Reklamation – complaint
Reklame – advertising
Repräsentant(in) – representative; (appointed) agent
reservieren – to book, reserve
Reservierung – booking
Rohmaterial – raw material
Rückerstattung – reimbursement
rumstöbern (im Internet ~) – to surf the Internet

S

Saldo – balance
Schaden – damage; defect
Schäden – damages
Schadensaufnahme – survey of damage
schätzen – to estimate
Schätzung – estimate; quotation
schicken – to send
Schiff (frei ~) – free on board
Schulden – debt(s)
Shareware – shareware
sicher sein – to be confident
Sichtwechsel – sight bill / draft
Soll – debit
Sonderpreis – special reduced price; preferential rate
Sortiment – range
sowie – together with
sowohl ... als auch – as well as
Sparkonto – deposit / savings account
Spediteur – carrier; forwarding agent

Spesen – expenses
Spezifikation – specification sheet
Stadtrand – outskirts
Stand – stand
Stand (auf den neuesten ~ gebracht) – updated
Standard – standard
Standardpreise – standard charges
Steigerung – increase
Stelle – job, post
Stelle (freie ~) – vacancy
Stichtag – deadline
Störung – disruption
stoßen (zufällig auf etw ~) – to come across sth
Strafe – fine
streichen – to cancel
Streik – strike
Stückpreis – unit price
Summe – amount, sum

T

Tarif – rate
technische(r) Berater(in) – technical adviser
technische Beschreibung – specification sheet
technischer Defekt – technical fault, breakdown
teilnehmen – to take part; to attend
Termin – appointment; deadline; date
Tippfehler – typing error
Treffen – meeting
treffen – to meet

U

überall in – throughout
überbelegen – to overbook
überbuchen – to overbook
Übereinkunft – agreement
übereinstimmen *(Zahlen, Berichte)* – to tally
Übereinstimmung (in ~ mit) – in accordance with
überfällig – overdue

Überprüfung (um e. ~ bitten) – to query

Übersee (in / nach ~) – overseas

übersteigen – to exceed

Überweisung – (credit) transfer; remittance

überzogen *(Konto)* – overdrawn

üblich – usual; standard

üblicher Postweg – snail mail

umfassend – wide

Umladekosten – handling charge

Umsatz – turnover

Umschlag – envelope

umsonst – free of charge

Unannehmlichkeit – inconvenience

unbefriedigend – unsatisfactory

unbesetzt – unoccupied, vacant

unerledigt – outstanding

unglücklich sein – to be unhappy, distressed

Unkosten haben – to incur expenses

unsachgemäße Verpackung – inadequate packing

Unstimmigkeit – discrepancy

unten erwähnt – undermentioned

Untergestell *(für Telefon)* – stand

Unterkunft – accommodation

unterschreiben – to sign

unterstreichen – to underline

Untersuchung (bei näherer ~) – upon investigation

unterzeichnen – to sign

unverkäuflich – unsaleable; not negotiable

unwesentlich – slight, irrelevant, unimportant

V

Verabredung – appointment

Verabredung (e. ~ einhalten) – to keep an appointment

veranlassen – to arrange

Veranstaltung – event

verarbeiten – to process

verbessern – to improve

verbindliches Angebot – firm offer

Verbindung – connection, link

Verbindung (sich in ~ setzen mit) – to contact

Verbraucher(in) – consumer

verbunden – obliged

vereinbart (wie ~) – as arranged

verfügbar – available

Verfügbarkeit – availability

verhandeln über – to negotiate

Verkäufe – sales

Verkäufer(in) – seller; salesperson

Verkaufsabteilung – sales department

Verkaufsleiter(in) – sales manager

Verkaufsstrategie – sales policy

Verladen – loading

verlangen – to demand; to require; to stipulate

verlängern – to extend; to renew

Verlängerungskabel – extension wire / lead

verlässlich – reliable

Verlust – loss

Vermerk – note

Verpackung – packing

Versammlung – meeting

Versand – dispatch / despatch; distribution; consignment

versäumen(,) etw zu tun – to fail to do sth

verschieben – to adjourn, postpone, put off *(informal)*

verschiffen – to ship

Verschiffung – shipment

Versenden – consignment

Versender – consignor

Versicherer – insurer, underwriter

Versicherung – insurance

Versicherung (durch e. ~ gedeckt sein) – to be covered by insurance

Versicherung (e. ~ abschließen) – to take out an insurance policy

Versuch – trial

vertagen – to adjourn

Vertrag – contract

Vertreter – agent
Vertreter(in) – representative
Vertretervertrag – agency agreement
Vertrieb – sales; sales department
Vertriebsgesellschaft – distribution company
verzögern – to delay
Verzögerung – delay
verzollt (geliefert ~) – delivery duty paid
viel versprechend – promising, encouraging
Vierteljahr – quarter
vierteljährlich – quarterly
Vollmacht – warrant
Vollpension – full board
Voraus (im ~) – in advance
vorausgehend – prior
Vorauszahlung – advance payment; cash in advance
vorbehaltlich – subject to
Vorbereitungen treffen – to make arrangements
vorhaben (etw ~) – to have sth on
vorhaben etw zu tun – to intend to do sth
vorhergehend – previous
vorherige Benachrichtigung – prior notice
vorlegen – to submit
vorrätig (etw ~ haben) – to have sth in stock
Vorschlag – suggestion, proposal
vorschlagen – to suggest, propose
Vorsitzende(r) – chairman, -woman, -person
vorstellen (jdm etw ~) – to point out sth to sb; to show sb sth
vorteilhaft – beneficial

W

Wachstum – growth; increase
Wahl (in die engere ~ kommen) – to be short-listed
Währung – currency

Ware(n) – goods
Warensendung – shipment
Wartungsingenieur(in) – maintenance engineer
Webseite – web page
Wechsel – bill (of exchange); draft
Wechselkurs – exchange rate
wegen – owing / due to
weit – wide
weiter – further
weiterleiten – to pass on; to forward
Werbekampagne – advertising campaign
Werbeveranstaltung – promotion
Werbung – advertising
Werk – factory
Werk (ab ~) EXW (ex works)
Werkstatt – workshop
Wert – value
Wettbewerb – competition
wettbewerbsfähig – competitive
wie ... erwähnt – as mentioned
wiegen – to weigh
Wirtschaftsjahr – financial year
Wirtschaftsprüfer(in) – accountant, auditor
Wunsch (auf ~ erhältlich) – available upon request; optional
Wünsche – wishes

Z

Zahlung nach Warenerhalt – charges forward
Zahlungsaufschub – extension of payment time, respite
Zahlungsbedingungen – terms / conditions of payment
Zahlungsmitteilung – advice of payment
Zahlungsunfähigkeit – failure to pay
Zeit (die ganze ~ über) – throughout
Zeitplan – schedule
Zentrale – head office
zerbrochene Ware – breakages
Zimmer (leeres ~) – vacancy

Zoll(polizei) – customs
Zollabfertigung – customs clearance
zollfrei – duty free
Zollgebühren – customs duties
zollpflichtig – dutiable
Zubehör(-teil) – accessory; component part
zugeben – to admit
zunehmen – to increase
zurück an den Absender – return to sender

zurückerstatten – to refund
zurückgeben – to return, give back
zurückschicken – to return, send back
zusammen mit – together with
zusätzlich – additional, further
zuversichtlich – confident
zuzüglich berechnen – to charge at extra cost
zwanglose Kleidung – casual dress
Zweigstelle – branch
Zwischenverkauf – prior sale